Economic Geographies of Globalisation

This book is dedicated to my son Tom

Economic Geographies of Globalisation

A Short Introduction

Martin Sokol

Visiting Research Fellow, School of Geography, Queen Mary, University of London and Senior Lecturer in Geography, Department of Geographical and Life Sciences, Canterbury Christ Church University, Canterbury, UK

Edward Elgar
Cheltenham, UK • Northampton, MA, USA

Published by
Edward Elgar Publishing Limited
The Lypiatts
15 Lansdown Road
Cheltenham
Glos GL50 2JA
UK

Edward Elgar Publishing, Inc.
William Pratt House
9 Dewey Court
Northampton
Massachusetts 01060
USA

A catalogue record for this book
is available from the British Library

Library of Congress Control Number: 2011925782

ISBN 978 1 84980 149 2 (cased)
ISBN 978 1 84980 153 9 (paperback)

Typeset by Servis Filmsetting Ltd, Stockport, Cheshire
Printed and bound by MPG Books Group, UK

Contents

Figures

Boxes

Acknowledgements

Much of the material in the book, while drawing on my research, has been developed while teaching various economic geography courses at Queen Mary, University of London (QMUL), University College London (UCL), University of Connecticut (UConn London Programme) and Canterbury Christ Church University (CCCU). I am grateful to all my students for their feedback and comments.

The draft of this book was originally written as a Subject Guide for the External Programme of the University of London (published by University of London Press in 2009). Roger Lee and Nigel Spence at QMUL and Steve Gibbons at the London School of Economics (LSE) read early drafts of my manuscript as part of a thorough review process. I am indebted to Roger, Nigel and Steve for their encouragement, suggestions and comments, all of which improved the quality of the draft. I would also like to thank Rosie Gosling, Director of External Study, and Kate Barker at LSE for their support and advice during the writing process of the Subject Guide.

I am forever grateful to all my colleagues at QMUL for their encouragement, support and collegial environment without which this book would have not been born. I am particularly indebted to the members of the Economy, Development and Social Justice research group, namely Adrian Smith, Jane Wills, Cathy McIlwaine, Kavita Datta, Alastair Owens, Konstantinos Melachroinos, Jon May and Al James, in addition to Roger Lee and Nigel Spence already mentioned. Al is also thanked for providing a photograph of an advertisement in India for Chapter 7 and for being the best co-pilot when driving on the memorable Los Angeles fieldtrip led by legendary Jon. Beyond the immediate research group I would like to thank Bronwyn Parry, Alison Blunt, Miles Ogborn, Catherine Nash, Simon Reid-Henry, David Pinder, Tim Brown, Tim Heinemann and many others. Ed Oliver contributed his excellent cartographic skills to the production of Figures 4.3 and 4.4. Thanks to Marta, Helen, Eszter and Jenny for keeping an eye on me. Finally, Walter Bertoldi is being thanked and congratulated for making the best pizzas in the entire Victoria Park village and probably the world.

I would also like to thank my CCCU colleagues, namely, Dan Donoghue,

Alex Kent, Julia Maxted, Peter Vujakovic, Chris Young, John Hills and Jaimie Miller, for making me feel at home.

At Edward Elgar Publishing, I am grateful to Felicity Plester for enthusiastically embracing the book proposal, to Laura Seward for patiently waiting for the final manuscript to arrive and to Jo Betteridge and her colleagues for safely navigating the book through the editing and production processes. Two anonymous reviewers kindly provided their comments on the first draft and I am grateful for these. The book took on a new structure and saw important improvements as a consequence. Also, several new case studies have been added, further improving the manuscript. The ongoing financial and economic crisis provided me with additional impulses and reassurances that writing this book was a worthwhile project. I am thus metaphorically indebted to the global economy for providing me with such fascinating material to write about.

Finally, many thanks to my son Tom, who was born – completely unaware – amid the worst global financial and economic crisis in living memory, and who is a constant source of strength and inspiration.

Abbreviations

AFTA	ASEAN Free Trade Area
APS	Advanced producer services
ASEAN	Association of South East Asian Nations
BRIC	Brazil, Russia, India and China (emerging markets)
CBD	Central business district
EU	European Union
FDI	Foreign direct investment
GATS	General Agreement on Trade in Services
GATT	General Agreement on Tariffs and Trade
GDP	Gross domestic product
GNP	Gross national product
ICT	Information and communication technology
ILO	International Labour Organization
IMF	International Monetary Fund
IT	Information technology
KIBS	Knowledge-intensive business services
LDC	Less developed country
LETS	Local exchange trading systems
LLDC	Least developed country
LLW	London living wage
MBS	Mortgage-backed securities
MNC	Multi-national corporation (or company)
NAFTA	North American Free Trade Agreement
NEG	New Economic Geography (Krugman-style)
NGO	Non-governmental organisation
NIC	Newly industrialised country
NIDL	New international division of labour
NMW	National minimum wage
OECD	Organisation for Economic Co-operation and Development
PIGS	Portugal, Ireland, Greece and Spain
PPP	Purchasing power parity
PPS	Purchasing power standards
R&D	Research and development
TNC	Trans-national corporation (or company)

UK	United Kingdom
UN	United Nations
US	United States
US$	US dollar
USSR	Union of Soviet Socialist Republics
WB	World Bank
WTO	World Trade Organization
WWII	The Second World War

Introduction

This book is a small contribution to a big debate about economic globalisation. It provides a compact introduction to key theoretical approaches that help us to understand how economies work, why they suffer recessions and crises and why economic inequalities at various levels are growing in the context of globalisation. The book will be of interest to all those who want to know more about the process of economic globalisation itself and complex geographies, inequalities and instabilities it brings about.

In my mind, the issues of inequality and instability have always been important for the 'global' economy. But their importance has been further highlighted by the financial and economic crisis that recently shook the global economy. This worst economic disaster in a generation has ongoing ramifications around the world for the lives of millions of people, probably including your own. The need for a debate about a more balanced, more equitable and more stable economic development framework has never been greater. The book thus links theoretical insights with the real examples of processes in the contemporary global economy and policy challenges these processes generate.

This book has been specifically written for students and readers with an interest in geography, economics, finance, business and management studies, planning, politics, development studies and social sciences more broadly. Both undergraduate and postgraduate students in globalisation studies will find chapters of this book particularly useful. I took great care to write this book in an accessible language. Theory is explained step by step and even readers with little prior knowledge will be able to understand fairly complex concepts. This opens the readership of this book well beyond academic campuses. I hope that you will find *Economic Geographies of Globalisation* useful whether you are a student or researcher, practitioner or policy-maker or simply a concerned citizen.

I have written this book from a critical economic geography perspective. Economic geography is a subject that employs a geographical approach to provide insights and understanding of the economy. Some people think that economic geography is about describing economies of individual countries or the location of their industries. A common misunderstanding is that in the globalising world, geography simply does not matter anymore since firms can locate anywhere around the globe. Some believe that geographical distance is 'dead' and that we are witnessing the 'end of geography'. However, as economic activities are increasingly internationalised, interconnections between various places increase, competition between them intensifies and inequalities are on the rise, so geography becomes more important than ever. Thus, the question of 'how economies work over space' becomes crucial for our understanding of economic globalisation. In other words, economic geographies of globalisation provide a key for understanding economic processes around us.

Given this, I believe that the book is also relevant for many actors in both the public and the private spheres including local, regional and national authorities, international bodies, non-governmental organisations or private consultancies, especially in the area of local and regional development, planning, business and economic development, both in the so-called 'developed' Global North and 'developing' countries of the Global South. I hope that economists and business leaders alike will find insights from economic geography useful.

What readers will hopefully take away from this book is an understanding of economic geography as a dynamic, diverse and contested body of knowledge that aims to provide critical insights into the workings of contemporary societies and economies. The book will introduce you to basic approaches, concepts and theories that economic geographers use; it will help you to understand how these concepts and theories may be applied in the context of the globalising world economy; and it will make you aware of the ways in which economic geography approaches can inform policy-making.

I have written this book with a strong conviction that only a thorough understanding of the workings of the economy can help us make informed policy choices. But there is still a lot that we do not know about economies and their geographies. There are still huge question marks hanging over the recent global financial and economic crisis. There are massive policy dilemmas ahead. This book is not intended to give simple answers to complex questions. If you are looking for simple policy fixes, please buy a different book.

However, if reading *Economic Geographies of Globalisation* will make you think more critically about economic processes around us, then I will feel that my efforts were worthwhile. In addition, I hope that reading my book will also prompt you to want to know, and to read, more. There are several other relevant books available. Many of these are excellent in their own right and I provide pointers to these in the lists of Further Reading that accompany each of the chapters. I believe that *Economic Geographies of Globalisation* will provide you with solid foundations on which to build, thus making it easier to read more challenging texts and to engage with some important academic and policy debates of our time.

I divided the book into eight chapters. Chapter 1 serves as an introduction to the key issues of economic globalisation. The chapter first outlines the extent of inequalities in the contemporary global economy, before discussing the recent global financial and economic crisis. Inequality and the crisis of the global economy in turn raise important questions about how economies work and how they work over space. The chapter will argue that economic geography is well placed to elucidate these questions.

Chapter 2 then moves on to explain what economic geography is. The chapter will highlight the importance and relevance of economic geography for analysing the global economy and for addressing some of its pressing issues. The chapter introduces economic geography as a dynamic and diverse subject that has been shaped by a variety of theoretical approaches and intellectual traditions.

Chapter 3 then begins to examine these theoretical approaches and intellectual traditions in a bit more detail. Initially, the chapter addresses the question 'What is the economy?' before moving onto the question 'How does the economy work?'. The chapter focuses on three contrasting explanations of how economies work, namely, neo-classical, Marxist and evolutionary-institutionalist perspectives. The neo-classical approach emphasizes the self-correcting power of the 'invisible hand' of the market in producing economic equilibrium and a win–win situation. The Marxist approach, on the other hand, highlights the tendency of capitalist economies to produce booms and busts, while also creating social inequalities. Evolutionary-institutionalist views offer an alternative to the above two approaches, not least fuelled by a conviction that advanced economies are undergoing a transformation into knowledge-based economies.

Each of these three perspectives on the economy translates into a contrasting interpretation of the question 'How do economies work *over space*?'. These contrasting interpretations are then examined in more detail in subsequent chapters. Chapter 4 thus provides a foundation to the understanding of key concepts and theories derived from a neo-classical perspective. The concepts of neo-classical spatial equilibrium, location theory, central place theory and market potential will be discussed before turning to the concepts of agglomeration economies and cumulative causation. In doing so, the chapter will demonstrate that the expectation of market forces delivering some sort of harmonious spatial development may be problematic. Indeed, market forces themselves may contribute to aggravating inequalities in space.

Chapter 5 will provide insights into economic geography concepts and theories inspired by Marxist views. Key concepts such as circuits of capital, spatial fix, spatial divisions of labour and the core-periphery model will be introduced and explained. Reflecting the Marxist understanding of the economy, these concepts highlight the fact that uneven development over space is an unavoidable feature of any capitalist economy. Some of these concepts, in addition, also help us to understand the role geography plays in overcoming the tendency of capitalist economies towards crisis.

Chapter 6 will then discuss economic geography concepts associated with alternative economic perspectives, including the evolutionary-institutionalist perspective and the so-called 'new economic geography'. Among others, the chapter will introduce wave theories of technical and economic change; concepts of regional innovation systems and clusters; knowledge economies and learning regions; networks, trust and social capital; while also discussing the role of culture, ethnicity and gender in economies. All these concepts (often in striking contrast to both the neo-classical and Marxist approaches) provide us with additional insights into the question of how economies work over space.

Chapter 7 demonstrates how some of the concepts and theories introduced in previous chapters may apply to our contemporary globalising world. The themes covered will include geographies of economic globalisation (investment, production, trade, consumption); the issue of governing globalisation; trans-national and multi-national corporations (commodity chains and value networks); global finance; global cities and city-regions; geographies of ICT and knowledge economies; geographies of emerging and transition economies; and geographies of labour and migration.

Finally, Chapter 8 focuses specifically on the role economic geography may play in informing policy-making. It first introduces key policy responses to uneven development and economic development more generally, including neo-liberal approaches, Keynesian approaches, state-socialism, 'Third Way' and alternative economic approaches. The chapter then goes on to discuss policy dilemmas and challenges associated with economic globalisation, in particular those related to the issue of uneven development, inequality and instability of the global economy, while linking these with current policy debates in the wake of the global financial and economic crisis.

To illustrate the points made in the book, each chapter is accompanied by a wealth of figures, graphs, photographs and/or 'real-world' case studies. Further reading and further useful resources (websites) are also provided. I hope that you will enjoy reading this book.

Martin Sokol
London, 2010

1. Economic globalisation, inequality and instability

INTRODUCTION

The global financial and economic crisis that erupted in the final years of the 2000s is commonly considered as the worst economic disaster since the Great Depression of the 1930s. There is a shared sense that something has gone terribly wrong with the US and the global economies. The faith in the neo-liberal (free-market) economic model in general, and US-style capitalism in particular, has been shaken. The belief in neo-liberal globalisation and the benign effects that such globalisation was supposed to deliver has been undermined. In fact, there have been fears that globalisation (see Box 1.1) may go into reverse. One way or another, the crisis acted as a stark reminder that the processes of economic globalisation are accompanied by two major problems – growing inequality and growing instability of the globalising economy. Both these issues are subject to much controversy and contestation. Indeed, many people believe that globalisation is in fact helping to reduce poverty and inequalities around the world, while also making the global economy more stable. However, the available evidence (some of which is presented below) points largely to the opposite direction.

The chapter first engages with the question of what people and what places benefit or lose from economic globalisation. This is done by outlining broad patterns of inequality at various geographical scales, from global to local. The second part of the chapter discusses the issue of global instability, while focusing on the recent global financial and economic crisis. The chapter will end up suggesting that economic geography can offer useful insights into the workings of the global economy and shed some light on the causes of its inequality and instability.

BOX 1.1   GLOBALISATION

For many people globalisation simply means an increasing flow of information, people, goods and money across the globe, thanks to improving transport and telecommunications. In other words globalisation can be seen as the widening, deepening and speeding up of global interconnectedness (Held et al., 1999, p.14). However, it is important to stress from the outset that, despite being 'one of the most important ideas of our time' (Jones, 2006, p.17), the concept of globalisation is very much problematic and subject to debate (e.g., see Held and McGrew, 2003a). Indeed, as Held and his colleagues pointed out, globalisation 'lacks precise definition' and is in danger of becoming 'the cliché of our times' (Held et al., 1999, p.1). In their own attempt to define globalisation, Held and his colleagues refer to it as 'a process (or set of processes) which embodies a transformation in the spatial organization of social relations and transactions – assessed in terms of their extensity, intensity, velocity and impact – generating transcontinental or interregional flows and networks of activity, interaction, and the exercise of power' (ibid., p.16). By growing 'extensity' they mean the stretching of social, political and economic activities across frontiers, while growing 'intensity' refers to their intensification, or growing magnitude of flows and interconnectedness. 'Velocity' is basically the speed with which global interactions are happening, while the 'impact' implies 'a deepening enmeshment of the local and global' such that the impact of distant events 'is magnified while even the most local developments may come to have enormous global consequences' (ibid., p.15). Taken together, these processes potentially represent a dramatic change in our appreciation of time and space, for many believe that globalisation is making the world smaller and that societies (and economies) are somehow coming closer together.

Indeed, many people believe that globalisation is dramatically reducing the importance of geography or bringing about the 'end of geography' altogether. But as is demonstrated in this chapter and throughout the book, globalisation is in itself an uneven process (or set of processes) unfolding differently in different geographical contexts and scales and having very different impacts on different people and places. Indeed, as Held and McGrew (2003b, p.4) have noted, 'a significant segment of the world's population is either untouched directly by globalisation or remains largely excluded from its benefits'. It is therefore not surprising that glo-balisation 'is arguably a deeply divisive and, consequently, vigor-ously contested process' (ibid.). The imperative to better understand the process of globalisation has been further exacerbated by the latest global financial and economic crisis that destroyed lives and livelihoods of many millions of people around the world.

INEQUALITY IN THE GLOBAL AGE

Global Inequalities

Global inequalities of wealth are massive and increasing. A simple way of looking at these inequalities is through the lens of the '80:20' rule (see, e.g. Regan, 2002). Such a rule suggests that 20 per cent of the world's population living in the highest-income countries control over 80 per cent of world income (Dicken, 2007, p.441). Conversely, this means that the remaining 80 per cent of the world's people living in 'developing' countries receive less than 20 per cent of the world's income. The '80:20' rule is just a rule of thumb, but it gives us a good sense of the scale of inequalities between the 'Global North' and the 'Global South' (sometimes referred to as the global North–South divide). However, the 80:20 split is perhaps an underestimation of the real inequalities, which are growing at a fast pace.

Indeed, it has been estimated that in 1960, the richest 20 per cent of the world's population received 70 per cent of global income. By 1980 this share of income increased to 76 per cent. By the end of the twentieth century, the richest fifth of the world's population received 90 per cent of global income. This concentration of wealth has been coupled with a decreasing share of global wealth received by the poorest 20 per cent of the world's population. Indeed, in 1960 the poorest fifth of the world's popu-lation received 2.3 per cent of global income. By 1980, this share decreased to 1.7 per cent. By the end of the twentieth century, the bottom fifth's share of global income shrank further to 1.4 per cent (Ellwood, 2001, p.101). The result is a staggering increase in inequality. Indeed, the ratio of the income of the world's richest 20 per cent of the population to the income of the world's poorest 20 per cent stood at 30:1 in 1960. By 1980, the ratio grew to 45:1 and by the year 2000, the income disparity ratio increased dramatically to 70:1 (Potter et al., 2004, p.36). This reflects a growing share of the world's richest nations of global income.

This does not automatically mean that the poor nations are getting poorer. Indeed, United Nations' *Human Development Report 2001* has noted with some optimism that the situation among the nations of the developing world has in fact been improving thanks to 'impressive gains' achieved in the last three decades of the twentieth century (UNDP, 2001, p.10). The report has argued that 'many more people can enjoy a decent standard of living' in developing countries, where income 'almost doubled in real terms between 1975 and 1998' (ibid.). However, behind this general picture 'lies a more complex picture of diverse experiences' across countries, macro-regions and groups of people (ibid.). In other words, the geography of this purported success is highly uneven. Indeed, while it is claimed that all macro-regions 'have made progress in human development in the past 30 years', they have been 'advancing at very different paces and achieving very different levels' (ibid.). Undeniably, there are noticeable differences between macro-regions. The least progress (if any) has been achieved in Sub-Saharan Africa and among the least developed countries (LLDCs). Meanwhile, the most impressive improvements among the macro-regions of the Global South, have been achieved by the East Asia and the Pacific macro-region (ibid.), although commencing from a very low starting point. There are also important differences within macro-regions (see also below) and some countries did better than others.

It is important to recognise, however, that much of the progress achieved in East Asia can be attributed to China and its fast economic advance (see also discussion on emerging economies in Chapter 7). China also contributed to a significant reduction in the number of people living in extreme poverty (e.g., see UNDP, 2007, p.24). Some would argue that this is an example of a successful impact of globalisation. It is true that China's economic growth has been mostly based on exports to the rest of the world, that is, directly linked to globalisation. However, as Nobel Prize-winning economist Joseph Stiglitz (2007, p.10) argues, China 'managed globalization carefully'. To put it differently, China has not followed the neo-liberal globalisation that many pro-market commentators have been advocating. Indeed, as Stiglitz argues, China was, for instance, 'slow to open up its own markets for imports, and even today does not allow the entry of hot speculative money' (ibid.). The success of China in reducing poverty through this managed globalisation is hard to dispute.

However, regardless of an 'impressive progress' in development achieved by many countries, 'unacceptable levels of deprivation in people's lives' can be seen still across the world (UNDP, 2001, p.9). Indeed, there are 'still around 1 billion people living at the margins of survival on less

than US$1 a day, with 2.6 billion – 40 per cent of the world's population
– living on less than US$2 a day' (UNDP, 2007, p.25). Furthermore, these
figures need to be seen in the context of global population dynamics. As
Stiglitz (2007, p.10) explains, the world has been 'in a race between economic growth and population growth, and so far population growth is
winning'. Therefore, 'even as the percentage of people living in poverty
is falling, the absolute number is rising' (ibid.). However, if we exclude
China, poverty in the Global South has in fact increased in both absolute
and relative terms in the last couple of decades (ibid., p.11).

In the meantime, high-income economies – mostly members of the
Organisation for Economic Co-operation and Development (OECD) such
as the US, Canada, Australia, Japan and most European countries – have
improved their economic position in the last three decades of the twentieth
century. The net effect is that the gap in absolute income levels between
the world's macro-regions has widened (Figure 1.1; UNDP, 2001, p.17;
Potter et al., 2004, p.35). Of course, income is not everything. Indeed,
there is an important debate about the way poverty, human well-being
and development should be measured and understood (e.g., see Chant and
McIlwaine, 2009). More widely, there is a debate to be had about the way
economy is defined and measured (see Chapter 3). However, it is important to acknowledge that different levels of income may reflect very different living standards and life chances. It remains to be seen what impact the
global financial and economic crisis will have on global inequalities. While
it is true that high-income countries have been badly shaken, one can fear
that economies of the Global South are more vulnerable and less able to
withstand the economic turmoil. The crisis can therefore reverse any previous gains achieved in terms of eradicating poverty and can reinforce the
pattern of global inequality.

Inequalities Within Macro-regions

Having said all this, it is important to recognise that important inequalities and diverging economic pathways exist within the world's macro-
regions themselves (Dicken, 2007, pp.64–7). Indeed, even in the most
prosperous macro-regions of the Global North, not everybody is well-
off. Europe is a case in point. The European economy is one of the
wealthiest macro-regions in the world. However, within Europe itself,
processes of economic convergence and divergence are in operation at
various geographical scales (Dunford and Smith, 2000), creating a very
uneven economic landscape. In other words, economic geography of
Europe is a complex affair. In simplest terms, however, the following
macro-regional pattern can be identified. The European economic space

GDP per capita (1985 PPP US$)

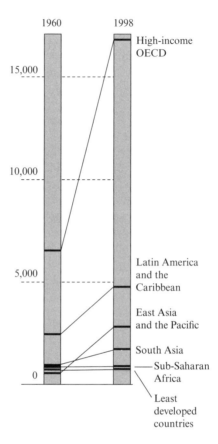

Source: UNDP (2001, p.17).

*Figure 1.1   Widening income gap between macro-regions, measured as
            purchasing power parity (PPP)*

appears to have its distinctive 'core' – Western Europe's major economic
'growth axis' – stretching from London and South-East England through
Belgium, Netherlands and Germany to Switzerland and Northern Italy
(Dicken, 2007, pp.64–5). This economic core could be seen as sur-
rounded by a 'centre' and 'periphery' each representing a very different
level of economic development. Meanwhile in the East lies what can be
defined as Europe's 'super-periphery' (Sokol, 2001) creating a very clear
East–West divide (see Figure 1.2). The super-periphery comprises former

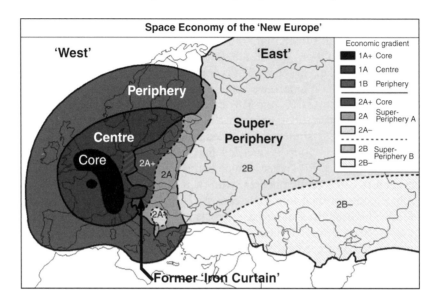

Source: Adapted from Sokol (2001).

Figure 1.2   Space economy of the European macro-region

state-socialist countries, once separated from the West by the so-called 'Iron Curtain'.

Following the collapse of state-socialism in the late 1980s, an opportunity has arisen for the unification of the divided continent. Nations of Central and Eastern Europe opted for forms of a liberal market economy in a bid to catch up economically with their Western European counterparts. However, following years of painful transformation from centrally planned state-socialist economies to market-led capitalist forms of development, it has become clear that the process is far more complex than expected (see also Chapter 8 for a discussion). The economic convergence with the West has proved to be difficult. After the first decade of transformation, the super-periphery as a whole was worse off and the gap with Western Europe has widened. However, there have been major differences within the super-periphery. Most notably, economies of East-Central Europe (former satellites of the Soviet Union) fared much better than the former Soviet Union itself. Further differences can be found within these two groups. As a result of these diverging economic performances, a profound fragmentation of the European economic space has occurred (Sokol, 2001). It is true that after the initial difficulties several economies of Central and Eastern

Europe experienced dynamic growth. Even so, the differences in wealth in Europe remain substantial.

This differentiation within the European economic space is clearly visible when looking at the level of economic development measured at the country level. The standard way of doing this is to measure so-called gross domestic product (GDP), normally calculated as GDP per capita (i.e., per inhabitant). To better compare the standards of living between individual countries, GDP is sometimes re-calculated at purchasing power parity (PPP) or, what in Europe is called purchasing power standards (PPS). GDP per capita at PPS reflects much better what inhabitants in a particular country can actually purchase with their income (and regardless of the exchange rate of their home currencies). This reflects the living standards of individual countries more accurately (since lower-income countries may be compensated for by cheaper goods and services available in a given country). However, even when looking at per capita GDP figures measured at PPS, it is clear that a massive wealth gap exists in Europe between the richest country (Luxembourg) and the poorest one (Bulgaria) (Figure 1.3).

The way in which GDP is calculated will be explained later in Chapter 3. However, it will also be argued there that measuring economies in this way can be highly problematic. Indeed, GDP reflects a rather narrow definition of what represents an economy. This is an important point and deserves further attention (see Chapter 3 for a discussion). But for now let's accept that the inequality of income as measured by GDP reflects massive gaps in standards of living in Europe. Again, it will be interesting to see to what extent the global financial and economic crisis will impact on this pattern of inequality within Europe. So far the signs are that the impact of the crisis will be harder in weaker economies of the European periphery and super-periphery (see also discussion below), which may further reinforce the pattern of existing inequality.

Inequalities Within Countries

Beyond the macro-regional disparities presented above, a more detailed examination reveals that major inequalities exist *within* individual countries (nation-states). These inequalities have both social and spatial dimensions. Social inequality can be measured in a number of ways, but usually it is expressed through an indicator of income inequality called Gini coefficient (Gini coefficient of 0 = perfect equality, i.e., the wealth is evenly distributed between all citizens; 100 = total inequality, i.e., one person owns everything). As the United Nations' *Human Development Report 2001* notes, there are 'vast' variations in the level of intra-country inequality, with Gini coefficients 'ranging from less than 20 in Slovakia to

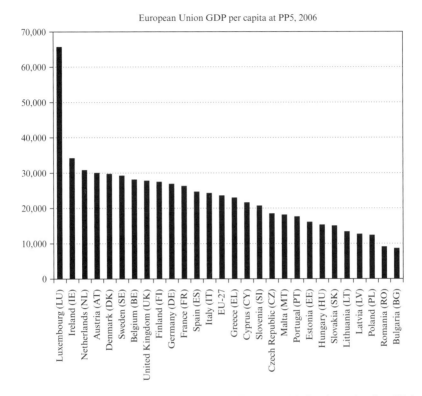

European Union GDP per capita at PP5, 2006

Source: Based on Eurostat data available at: http://europa.eu/abc/keyfigures/qualityoflife/index_en.htm.

Figure 1.3   GDP per capita in EU member states measured at purchasing power standards (PPS) in 2006

60 in Nicaragua and Swaziland' (UNDP, 2001, p.17). In general, income inequality is highest among the nations of Latin America, the Caribbean and Sub-Saharan Africa. South Asian countries are reported to have 'fairly low' Gini coefficients, in the 30s. Most countries in East-Central Europe and the former Soviet Union have relatively low inequality, perhaps reflecting the legacy of egalitarian policies followed under state-socialism (see Chapter 8). Having said that, 'transition' to capitalism has been accompanied by growing social inequalities, most notably in Russia where income inequality has increased dramatically since the collapse of state-socialism (ibid., p.18). Among the advanced OECD economies, the highest levels of income inequality can be found in the United Kingdom and the United States, the beacons of Anglo-Saxon neo-liberal capitalism.

Meanwhile, Austria and Scandinavian countries such as Denmark have the lowest levels of income inequality (ibid.). As we shall see in Chapter 8, low levels of social inequalities may be associated with particular economic policies adopted by individual countries.

Another aspect of intra-country inequality deserving our attention relates to *spatial* inequalities. As subsequent chapters of this book will make abundantly clear, economic processes are unfolding across space in an uneven way. In other words, geography matters. Spatial inequality within a country reflects the unevenness of economic processes on its territory. Again, this can be measured in various ways, but perhaps the most common (if problematic) way of measuring spatial inequality within a country is to consider differences in *regional* GDP. Comparing the economic level of individual regions in this way will reveal the extent of uneven development among regions (so-called 'regional disparity'). Several problems can arise while doing this, one of which is a delineation of meaningful statistical boundaries for which to collect data. For instance, mass commuting around a major city may distort its regional GDP per capita if boundaries around the city are too tightly defined. If this occurs, economic activities that commuters perform in the city are counted in the regional GDP, but commuters themselves are not included in the count of the population of the city. As a consequence of this, the regional GDP per capita figure for that city is statistically inflated at the expense of the city's hinterland. Therefore, regional GDP per capita figures need to be treated with care (especially those involving big urban centres).

An alternative way of measuring spatial inequality is to consider disposable income of the inhabitants of a given region, but these figures are not always available for all countries. Various other ways exist through which spatial inequalities can be expressed (e.g., levels of regional unemployment, social deprivation, business start-ups, etc.). Whichever indicator is being used (or a combination of indicators) it can help us to establish the extent of uneven regional development within a country. The key point here is that even the most advanced economies in the world display significant regional disparities (e.g., see Pike et al., 2006; Dicken, 2007, pp.482–6). These regional inequalities, in turn, represent a form of 'social injustice' in that 'unfairness of people's life chances and opportunities' are 'being shaped by where they live' (ibid., p.256).

The United Kingdom (UK) is a case in point. Regional GDP per capita figures vary greatly across the regions of the UK, revealing huge differences between the poorest parts of the country (North-East England) and the richest regions (London and South-East England). The persisting differences between the North and the South of the country led some commentators to suggest that the 'North–South divide' exists in Britain (see

-Martin, 1988, for an excellent discussion). However, an important point to remember is that people living in a 'wealthy' region do not necessarily share the same life chances and opportunities. In other words, the regional GDP per capita figure (or any other spatial indicator) may mask substantial inequalities *within* regions. Nowhere else is this more visible than in global cities, which we will consider in turn.

'Local' Inequalities in Global Cities

Global cities, such as London, New York or Tokyo, are perhaps the richest places on earth when measured by GDP per capita. This is a reflection of a massive concentration of high-value economic activities they attract (see also Chapter 7 for a discussion). However, the fact that a region or a city has a high regional GDP per capita does not necessarily mean that all its inhabitants are well-off. Far from it! Indeed, through the processes we will discuss in Chapter 7, it appears that global cities are characterised by increasing income polarisation of its inhabitants. On the one hand, there are wealthy elites and 'super-rich' who earn fortunes working in finance and other advanced business services; on the other, there is a growing army of people who struggle to simply survive (Figure 1.4). The latter group of people are often unemployed or rely on a variety of precarious, low-skill, low-paid service jobs. The irony is that some of these jobs (e.g., cleaning services or security services) are directly servicing the very businesses of the super-rich. More generally, it could be argued that it is only thanks to the work of thousands of these low-paid workers that global cities, such as London, can function (see Box 1.2). Without these workers, urban transport, catering services, or the hospitality industry, for instance, could hardly work (e.g., May et al., 2007; Wills et al., 2009). Yet the wealth generated in global cities fails to 'trickle down' from the rich to the poor. Thus, massive inequalities exist within global cities and thousands of their inhabitants experience living and working conditions that very much resemble those found in the developing world. In this way, global cities can comprise the elements of both the Global North and the Global South in one place, bringing together both the top earners of the planet as well as those least well off. In addition to this, various other forms of inequality, for example, those based on gender, race or ethnicity, are apparent in global cities (see, for example, Hamnett, 2003). Global cities, in other words, represent a micro-cosmos of the unequal world that we live in. Global cities are therefore also places from which one can start to unravel inequalities of social relations – an effort that perhaps requires us to go beyond the simple notion of 'territorial inequalities' as measured by GDP. As will be shown later in the book, economic geography can provide

Source: Photo by Martin Sokol.

Figure 1.4   Inequality in a global city: homeless man in the streets of New York, one of the richest places on earth

useful insights into both spatial and relational inequalities. Equally, an economic-geographical approach can be helpful in analysing the causes and consequences of economic instability, to which we now turn.

INSTABILITY OF THE GLOBAL ECONOMY

Not so long ago, many prominent economists thought that the repeat of an economic crisis of the scale of the Great Depression was impossible. Paul Krugman, the Nobel Prize-winner in economics, has described nicely how his fellow US economists had thought that the 'central problem of depression-prevention' had been solved (see Krugman, 2008, p.9). Not that those economists would necessarily think that the economic fluctuations (also known as 'business cycles') were eradicated altogether, but there was a strong belief that a modern macroeconomic policy had

BOX 1.2   LONDON: GLOBAL CITY, LOCAL INEQUALITY

London is one of the richest and most important global cities and one of the key sites of globalisation (Sassen, 2001; Massey, 2007). Importantly, London is also one of the biggest financial centres in the world, anchored mostly in the traditional financial quarter, 'the City', in the heart of London and its more recent extension in Canary Wharf in East London (Figure 1.5). Investment decisions made in London influence the fate of companies and whole countries around the world, while events in faraway places influence the fortunes of the financial centre. In this sense, tentacles of finance illustrate well one of the aspects of globalisation (cf. Box 1.1). Billions of pounds, dollars and euros flow through London every day, with the financial industry employing a growing professional and managerial class (Hamnett, 2003). Some of the bankers and financiers working in London can easily be classed as 'super-rich', enjoying wages, benefits and bonuses whose value goes into millions of pounds per annum.

On the other hand, as the most recent research shows, London is also a home to a growing army of people employed in poorly paid jobs with no perks attached (May et al., 2007; Wills et al., 2009). Most of these people could in fact be classed as 'working poor' who fall within a 'wage gap' – a difference between a statutory minimum wage (i.e., the minimum wage required by the UK law) and a 'living wage' (i.e., a wage it is possible to live on). The wage gap is particularly pronounced in a global (and expensive) city like London. In 2008, for instance, just before the economic crisis started to bite, the national minimum wage (NMW) in the UK was set at £5.73 per hour, while the London living wage (LLW), that is, the wage that would guarantee a minimum acceptable quality of life in London, was calculated to be £7.45 per hour (see http://www.geog.qmul.ac.uk/livingwage/index.html*). The difference of £1.72 in hourly wages makes a huge difference to those involved. Workers falling within the wage gap are often forced to work long hours, unsociable hours or have multiple jobs to feed themselves and/or their families. It has been estimated that one in five workers in London may earn wages below the living wage (see May et al., 2007, p.154).

Low pay is often associated with extremely poor conditions of employment, with no overtime pay, sick pay, maternity leave, compassionate leave, company pension or holidays above the statutory minimum of 20 days (which includes bank holidays). Such jobs are mostly concentrated in London's 'elementary' positions such as cleaners, refuse collectors, porters, domestic workers or caretakers. Working in both public and private spheres (often via subcontracted agencies) this invisible army of people on poverty wages keeps the cities like London working. Indeed, London's transport system, hotels and restaurants, schools and hospitals, public institutions and private firms are reliant on their work. In fact, and ironically, those on poverty wages and those super-rich on multi-million bonuses can share the very same workplaces (without necessarily seeing each other).

Indeed, the offices of some of the world's most powerful financial institutions occupying the gleaming towers of the City of London and Canary Wharf need to be cleaned everyday by a small army of cleaners, many of whom are extremely poorly paid. In another twist of irony, many of these low-paid jobs are increasingly being done by foreign-born workers, further underlying the multifaceted nature of globalisation and extreme diversity of global cities such as London. It has been estimated that foreign-born workers now account for 29 per cent of London's total population and 35 per cent of London's working age population, while making up a disproportionate share (46 per cent) of London's low-paid workforce (ibid., p.155). Coming from all corners of the world (and often maintaining vital links with their homelands), these foreign-born migrant workers thus could be seen as representing another dimension of globalisation and a definition of London as a global city. Often being in the most vulnerable position in society, low-paid workers and foreign-born migrants have become a major focus of campaigns led by a broad-based community organisation called the London Citizens (part of Citizens UK), via the 'Living Wage' and 'Strangers into Citizens' campaigns. One can imagine that the challenges of low-paid workers will intensify as the full impact of the financial and economic crisis will hit all spheres of society.

* Last accessed 26 February 2011.

Source: Photo by Martin Sokol.

Figure 1.5   Global city, local inequality – London's Canary Wharf

'reduced the problem to the point that it was more of a nuisance than a front-rank issue' (ibid., p.10).

These sentiments have been echoed on the other side of the Atlantic. The former British Chancellor of the Exchequer (and later the Prime Minister), Gordon Brown, had famously declared at the time that the economic cycles of 'boom-and-bust' had been 'abolished'. It is therefore not surprising, that the global economic and financial crisis that struck in 2007–08 onwards took many economists and politicians by surprise. Amid the impressive economic growth of 1990s and 2000s in leading capitalist economies and indeed around the world, few expected that a disaster was around the corner.

But the economic disaster was waiting to happen. It started as a relatively minor 'blip' in the performance of financial products that few people outside banking circles had ever heard of before (so-called MBS – mortgage-backed securities) back in the summer of 2007. It subsequently evolved into a major 'credit crunch', causing a full-blown global financial crisis and resulting in a serious, synchronised global economic downturn. The biggest economy in the world, the US, where the trouble started, had been bracing itself for the worst economic crisis since the Great Depression of the 1930s. Once all-powerful and money-awash US banks have been facing massive losses and bankruptcies. Amid volatile financial markets, Lehman Brothers, one of the oldest and most powerful investment banks in the world, collapsed in September 2008, sending shockwaves throughout the financial world. The US federal government was forced to spend billions of dollars in bailouts to prevent the whole financial system from collapsing. Among the casualties of the turmoil was AIG, the biggest insurance company in the world, which had to be rescued by the government. Meanwhile, the rest of the US economy has been quickly sliding into a full-blown recession. The collapse of the housing market and a steep decline of economic activity translated into thousands of people losing their jobs, their houses or both. Amid the economic trouble, several economic sectors have been struggling to keep afloat. Car-makers, for instance, have been fighting for survival, as stocks of unsold cars started to pile up as a consequence of weakening consumer demand and difficult conditions in financial markets.

This bleak picture has been mirrored in other parts of the world. The crisis soon hit Europe. Ireland, a small open economy and previously the star economic performer reaping the benefits of globalisation, was the first EU member to go into recession (see also Box 7.2 in Chapter 7). Many other countries soon followed. *Recession* is a technical term describing a situation when an economy displays a negative growth for a period of at least two consecutive quarters. In other words, GDP is shrinking (not growing) for at least a half-year. This looks innocent enough, but can have serious consequences for people, business and governments. In the UK, several banks and mortgage lenders have nearly collapsed and the government had to step in and fully or part-nationalise some of them in order to prevent a major systemic financial failure. Despite these interventions, lending to households and firms has been curtailed, with knock-on effects for the rest of the economy. The housing market 'bubble' created during the boom years has burst and by 2009 hardly a day has passed without reports of further losses in the banking sector, a rapidly deteriorating economy and announcements of job redundancies across the country. The recession that accompanied this economic turmoil is considered one of the most severe in post-war history, with uncertain prospects for a full economic recovery (see also Chapter 8).

Similar difficulties have been seen in other major EU economies, be it France, Germany, Italy or Spain. However, it appears that the more peripheral economies (Portugal, Ireland, Greece and Spain – collectively also known by an ugly and unfair acronym 'PIGS') suffered more than others, perhaps with the exception of their East European counterparts. Indeed, the collapsing demand in the 'West', in turn, has wreaked havoc in Central and Eastern Europe, sending several economies of the region into a deep recession (e.g., see Gorzelak and Goh, 2010; Smith and Swain, 2010). Countries such as Latvia, Ukraine and Hungary had to accept massive loans from the International Monetary Fund (IMF) in order to stay afloat. Many households in the former state-socialist countries are now 'just one incident away from financial ruin' (Gill and Quillin, 2010, p.29; see also World Bank, 2010).

Asia, the third economic pillar of the global economy, has not been immune from the difficulties either. Global economic gloom compounded problems in Japan, which was already suffering a decade of stagnation. Meanwhile the prospects of Asian emerging economies, most notably India and China, have been badly shaken amid collapsing global trade.

The full scale of the impact is hard to predict at this stage, but it is becoming clear that economic fortunes and livelihoods of millions of people around the world will be affected by this global crisis. No matter where you are, in the Global North or Global South, East or West, I would expect that you can see around you (or experience) various direct and indirect consequences of this crisis. There is a growing realisation that 'the crisis has killed the myth of "happy" globalisation, in which everyone benefits' (see Thornhill, 2009, p.17).

It could be said that the crisis simultaneously killed a myth that advanced market economies are immune from crises. Indeed, as Paul Krugman (2008, p.3) reminds us, only several years ago many economists believed that the Great Depression of the 1930s was 'a gratuitous, unnecessary tragedy' and that 'nothing like the Great Depression can ever happen again'. The collapse of state-socialism in early 1990s further reinforced the faith in the capitalist economic system and by the turn of the century 'the world seemed more favourable to market economies than it had for almost ninety years' (ibid., p.10). But the confidence 'was misplaced' (ibid., p.5). Not that there was a lack of warning signs. In the late 1990s Asia experienced an economic downturn 'that bore an eerie resemblance to the Great Depression' (ibid., p.4). As Krugman (ibid.) describes, the Asian crisis 'sent chills up [his] spine'. And a careful look at history suggests that a crisis is a more endemic feature of an economy than we would like to think (e.g., Krugman, 2008; Reinhart and Rogoff, 2009). But it took depression-type problems to hit the US soil again for the topic of an economic crisis to be taken seriously. What has happened to the US and the world economy in the final years of the first decade of the twenty-first century has been labelled in various ways (see Box 8.1 in Chapter 8). Regardless of the labelling, however, most commentators agree that this is the biggest economic disaster since the Great Depression of the 1930s. And, as Howard Davies (2010, p.2) aptly put it, '[f]uture generations will be paying for this crisis for decades'.

CONCLUSION

To avoid future economic disasters like this and to make globalisation work for the benefit of people, there is an urgent need to understand the causes of both inequality and instability (and possible links between the two). More generally, there is a need to understand how economies work, don't work or should work. This, in turn, highlights the importance of several key issues that this book is concerned about. Indeed, the current global economic downturn highlights the need to understand, first and foremost, what 'the economy' is and how economies function (the two issues that will be explored in Chapter 3). Furthermore, there is a need to better understand how economies work *over space* (issues that will be explored in Chapters 4, 5 and 6) and, specifically, how economic processes work in the context of globalisation (Chapter 7). Finally, based on the knowledge of what people and what places benefit or lose from these economic processes, there is a need to reflect on how more stable, equitable and sustainable economies can be created (Chapter 8). In discussing all these issues, economic geography can provide some useful insights. So what is economic geography? This is the question that the following chapter will aim to answer.

FURTHER READING

On various aspects of globalisation
Ellwood, W. (2001) *The No-nonsense Guide to Globalization*. (London: Verso).
Held, D. and A. McGrew (eds) (2003) *The Global Transformations Reader: An Introduction to the Globalization Debate* (second edition). (Cambridge: Polity Press).
Held, D., A. McGrew, D. Goldblatt and J. Perraton (1999) *Global Transformations: Politics, Economics and Culture*. (Cambridge: Polity Press).
Jones, A. (2006) *Dictionary of Globalization*. (Cambridge: Polity Press).

On global inequalities

Chant, S. and C. McIlwaine (2009) *Geographies of Development in the 21st Century: An Introduction to the Global South.* (Cheltenham, UK and Northampton, MA, USA: Edward Elgar).

Potter, R.B., T. Binns, J.A. Elliot and D. Smith (2004) *Geographies of Development.* (Harlow: Pearson/Prentice Hall).

Stiglitz, J. (2002) *Globalization and its Discontents.* (London: Penguin).

Stiglitz, J. (2007) *Making Globalization Work.* (London: Penguin).

Wills, J., K. Datta, Y. Evans, J. Herbert, J. May and C. McIlwaine (2009) *Global Cities at Work: New Migrant Divisions of Labour.* (London and New York: Pluto Press).

On global instability

Ellwood, W. (2001) *The No-nonsense Guide to Globalization.* (London: Verso).

Gamble, A. (2009) *The Spectre at the Feast: Capitalist Crisis and the Politics of Recession.* (Basingstoke and New York: Palgrave Macmillan).

Krugman, P. (2008) *The Return of Depression Economics and the Crisis of 2008.* (London: Penguin).

USEFUL WEBSITES*

http://epp.eurostat.ec.europa.eu/portal/page/portal/eurostat/home – website of the Eurostat, the statistical office of the European Union, providing a wealth of information on inequalities at national and regional levels in Europe.

http://www.census.gov/ – website of the US Census Bureau, the statistical office of the United States.

http://www.citizensuk.org/ – website of the Citizens UK, a broad-based community organisation that leads, among others, 'The Living Wage' and the 'Strangers into Citizens' campaigns in London.

http://www.espon.eu/ – website of ESPON, the European Observation Network for Territorial Development and Cohesion, whose aim is to support policy development in relation to the aim of territorial cohesion and a harmonious development of the European territory.

http://www.geog.qmul.ac.uk/livingwage/index.html – website on the Living Wage campaign maintained by a group of geographers at Queen Mary, University of London, led by Professor Jane Wills.

http://www.globalpolicy.org/ – website of the Global Policy Forum, an independent policy watchdog that monitors the work of the United Nations and scrutinises global policy-making and the process of globalisation, including its implications for global inequalities.

http://www.sasi.group.shef.ac.uk/ – website of the Social and Spatial Inequalities (SASI) research group, led by Professor Danny Dorling and based at the Department of Geography, University of Sheffield, undertaking research on inequalities in the UK and globally. The SASI group is also behind the Worldmapper project (see below).

http://www.undp.org/ – website of the United Nations Development Programme.

http://www.worldmapper.org/ – website of the Worldmapper project created by the Social and Spatial Inequalities (SASI) group at the University of Sheffield, in collaboration with Mark Newman (University of Michigan). The website contains a wealth of data and several hundreds of maps on various aspects of the world, including numerous economic indicators.

* All accessed 26 February 2011.

2.   What is economic geography about?

INTRODUCTION

One of the key messages of this book is that critical economic-geographical perspectives can be helpful in our effort to better understand economies and the way they function. Some people may question whether geography can be helpful in analysing globalisation at all. Surely, globalisation, if anything, makes geography less relevant? However, as I will demonstrate in this chapter and throughout the book, geography has become ever more important as a result of globalisation. Indeed, the economic-geographical perspective emphasises that economies are always unfolding across space. In this sense 'there are no economies, only economic geographies' (Lee, 2006a, p.430). Critical economic-geographical perspectives thus help us to appreciate economic processes as intrinsically geographical to better understand their impacts on people and places. The process of globalisation itself is unfolding unevenly in space. Likewise, the global economic crisis has differentiated impacts on different people and places. Economic geography is thus well placed to get to grips with the pressing economic issues.

This chapter will introduce economic geography as a vibrant discipline that has a lot to offer in analysing contemporary societies and economies. 'What is economic geography?' is the first question that the chapter will aim to address. In doing so, it will introduce economic geography as a sub-discipline of geography that uses a geographical approach to study the economy. It will then go on to explain the key difference between the mainstream economics and economic-geographical perspectives on the economy. One of the key features and strengths of the economic-geographical approach is the use of the concepts of space, place and scale and these concepts will be introduced in turn. The chapter will also point out that economic geography itself represents a dynamic, evolving and diverse body of knowledge. However, this diversity also allows economic geography to engage with a number of issues in contemporary societies and economies. This also helps to answer the second question, which is 'Why is economic geography important?'. Indeed, despite the claims that economic globalisation will inevitably bring about 'the end of geography',

geography matters more than ever and economic geography provides us with useful tools to analyse and understand economic processes that shape our globalising world.

WHAT IS ECONOMIC GEOGRAPHY?

Economic geography is a sub-discipline that uses a geographical approach to study the economy. It is a vibrant and exciting branch of geography. Its name would suggest that economic geography lies somewhere between, or at the overlap of, the disciplines of geography and economics. This is true to some extent. In fact, both geographers and economists use the term 'economic geography'. However, they mean different things by it. Indeed, it is important to stress from the outset that the approach that geographers are using to study the economy is very different from that used by most economists.

This book uses the terms 'economic geography' and 'economic-geographical approach' to describe the approach used by geographers (see also Coe at al., 2007). On the other hand, the type of economic geography that economists are using, can be best described as 'geographical economics' (ibid., Preface, p.xx) or 'spatial economics'. More generally, this distinction between economic geography and geographical economics reflects fundamental differences between the way the economy is treated by geographers on the one hand, and economists on the other. In other words, an economic-geographical approach to studying the economy is very different from the one used by mainstream economics (see Figure 2.1). Let's have a look at these differences in more detail.

Key Differences Between Economic Geography and Economics Approaches

The key difference is that mainstream economists usually pay little attention to the geographical dimensions of economic processes while economic geographers consider geography as being essential for the understanding of the ways economies work. From this, two completely different views of the economy, and the way it operates, emerge.

Most mainstream economists see the economy as a machine that works according to certain principles and whose behaviour can be predicted using modelling techniques. Mathematics is therefore the main 'language' economists 'speak'. The body of thought that underpins such a conceptualisation of the economy can be referred to as 'economic

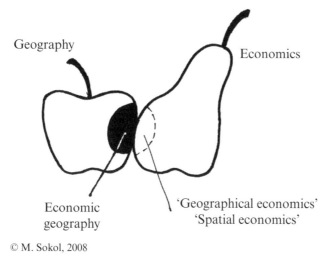

Geography

Economics

Economic geography

'Geographical economics'
'Spatial economics'

© M. Sokol, 2008

Source: Illustration by Martin Sokol.

Figure 2.1   Economic geography

orthodoxy'. Let us first explore the key components of economic orthodoxy before introducing the key concepts of an economic-geographical
perspective.

Mainstream economics (economic orthodoxy)
Key components of economic orthodoxy (see Coe et al., 2007, pp.10–11)
could be simply summarised as follows:

1. One of the key assumptions of economic orthodoxy is that all people
    are behaving in a rational, self-interested and economising, profit-
    maximising manner. This type of *rational* individual is sometimes
    referred to as 'economic man' or *homo economicus.*
2. Economic orthodoxy assumes that these rational individuals (directly
    or through firms) are competing against each other on the *market.*
    Mainstream (orthodox) economists believe that the market is the best
    mechanism to ensure economic efficiency since, they believe, perfect
    competition on the market guarantees that supply will meet demand
    at a particular price and the economy will be in *equilibrium.* The
    notion of equilibrium is one of the central assumptions of mainstream
    economic thought and shapes the way in which economists see the
    world around them.

3. Mainstream economists believe that the market economy operates according to certain *laws* and *principles* that could be studied as a 'science'. One of the main concerns of this economic science is to predict the behaviour of the economy using mathematical models and equations. The achievement of the aforementioned equilibrium is one of the key concerns of such modelling.
4. Mainstream economists believe that these laws and principles work everywhere and therefore economic models are applicable to them in every context. In other words, economic orthodoxy believes in certain *universalism*.

Some would argue that such a portrayal of economic orthodoxy is somewhat simplistic, a caricature of an increasingly diverse body of economics. However, a tendency among economists to assume some sort of universal applicability of basic economic 'laws' is rather pervasive. Within this world of universal laws there is little room for local differences and geography in general. Indeed, geography (with the exception of 'geographical economics') rarely enters economists' equations. The use of geography by economists is somewhat limited. There are some important exceptions, however. Among them is Paul Krugman, US economist and the Nobel Prize-winner for economics in 2008. Over the years, Krugman has made an important contribution in terms of bringing geography into economics and is seen as a leading figure of the so-called 'New Economic Geography' (NEG). However, his notion of geography is still somewhat limited and narrow, especially when compared with the conceptualisation of geography used by the economic-geographical perspective discussed below. Indeed, as you will see, there are stark differences between the 'New Economic Geography' used by economists and the 'new economic geography' used by geographers (see Box 2.1).

An economic-geographical perspective
In contrast to a rather limited appreciation of geography by most economists, geographers emphasise the fact that no economy can function at the head of a pin (Massey, 1995). In other words, 'all economies must *take place*' (Lee, 2006a, p.430, note 3; original emphasis). Geography, therefore, is always intrinsically present in all economic processes. One could therefore argue that, in fact, there are 'no economies, only economic geographies' (ibid.; see also Lee, 2002a).

It follows then, that the kind of universalism that mainstream economics assumes is somewhat problematic. Indeed, if all economic processes have a geographical dimension, then it is difficult to imagine that economic rules can apply equally to all places.

Homo economicus   Homo geographicus

© M. Sokol, 2008

Source: Illustration by Martin Sokol.

Figure 2.2   Homo economicus *and* Homo geographicus

Another major difference between an economic-geographical perspective and the assumptions of economic orthodoxy concerns the notion of a rational 'economic man' – *homo economicus*. As we have seen above, mainstream economists assume that people are always behaving as rational, profit-maximising individuals responding to market signals. However, life is more complex than that and people's behaviour is not always the outcome of rational decision-making. Rather, it can be influenced and conditioned by their gender, race, age, class, religion, culture, health or disability. Geographers are keen to take these aspects on board when studying economies. A 'geographical man/woman' – or what I will call here *homo geographicus* – can behave very differently from the way they are supposed to behave according to economic orthodoxy (see Figure 2.2).

This has important implications for the remaining assumptions of economic orthodoxy. Indeed, if people are not behaving in a predictable way, then it is hard to expect that the entire economy will behave according to some predictable laws and principles. However sophisticated, mathematical models may not be able to capture all the complexity of economic processes happening in the real world.

Worse still, mathematical models are not very helpful in elucidating the ways people relate to each other within societies and economies. In other words, 'the language of mathematics limits the ways in which economists can think about questions of *power* and *social relations*' (Lee, 2002a, p.20; emphasis added). However, the questions of power and social relations are crucial in understanding economies because people do not live and work in isolation. We are connected to each other in complex ways and economic geography helps us to explore these connections and relations. As we shall see later in this chapter, this exploration becomes *more* important in the age of globalisation.

Further to this, it could be argued that these connections and relations are not limited to market exchanges and transactions. Indeed, there is a wide range of economic processes happening outside the scope of the market. The diversity of forms of economic processes, both within and outside the scope of the market, means that many economic geographers are not talking about 'the economy' (singular) but about 'economies' (plural). In recent years, the notion of 'diverse' or 'alternative' economies attracted much interest among geographers (e.g., Lee and Wills, 1997; Lee, 2002b; Leyshon et al., 2003; Peck and Theodore, 2007). The notion of 'diverse economies' further undermines the universalism of economic orthodoxy and paves the way for alternative explanations of what the economy is and how it works.

Thus, one way or another, geographers in general, and economic geographers in particular, help to build a much richer, and perhaps more accurate, picture of the contemporary globalising economy. Coe and his colleagues go as far as to suggest that 'the set of approaches offered by the field of economic geography is best placed to help us appreciate and understand the modern economic world in all its complexity' (Coe et al., 2007, Preface, p.xviii). They identify the following key concepts that form part of the economic-geographical approach: space, place and scale. Let us examine these three concepts in more detail.

Key Concepts of Economic Geography: Space, Place and Scale

An economic-geographical approach puts spatial concepts such as space, place and scale at the centre of the analysis. These concepts form part of the common language that is shared among professional geographers (Coe et al., 2007, p.11). It is therefore essential that you familiarise yourself with these concepts right at the start:

Space
The concept of space refers to physical distance and area. The concept of space allows us to ask simple questions such as *where* a particular process is happening. Four interrelated elements of the concept of space can be identified:

- territoriality and form (e.g., a territorial form of a particular country);
- location (e.g., a location of a particular country);
- flows across space (e.g., trade flows between countries);
- the concept of uneven space as a necessary condition of a capitalist system (ibid., pp.14–15).

Place

The concept of place aims to capture the *specificity* or *uniqueness* of particular places that are carved out of space. Through the notion of place, geographers are able to explore the richness and complexity of particular places and economic processes that are always embedded in environmental, social, cultural, institutional and political contexts (ibid., pp.16–18). The idea of being embedded is very important because environmental, social, cultural, institutional and political contexts influence (and, in turn, are influenced by) economic processes. Many Western (occidental) values, for instance, may be alien to many other cultures, societies or nations. Therefore, the way economies are constructed and performed may be very different in different places (e.g., in London or in Trinidad). Despite its importance for geographical research, the notion of place is somewhat vague because it can take various shapes and sizes.

Scale

The concept of scale therefore helps us to organise places through a typology of spatial scales. Spatial scales that are commonly used by economic geographers include:

- global scale;
- macro-regional scale (e.g., South-East Asia, Europe or North America);
- national scale (e.g., US, UK, France, Niger, Japan);
- regional scale (e.g., California or South East of England);
- local scale (e.g., Silicon Valley, Manhattan or the City of London);
- lived places (e.g., workplaces and homeplaces) (ibid., pp.18–20).

It is worth noting that the precise typology is sometimes problematic. The terms 'local' and 'regional', for instance, are often used rather loosely. In some cases (e.g., Hong Kong, Singapore or Trinidad), it is difficult to establish whether we are looking at a national, regional or local scale (or a combination of these). So things are not always as simple as they look. When reading economic geography literature, you should always pay attention to what definition of scale a particular author is using.

Further to this, it is important to realise that the above three key concepts are not simply neutral tools for describing the world – they can also be seen as *representations* of the world. Indeed, the way these concepts are used by academics, the media or politicians influences the way we look at the world and how we understand its problems.

Major Theoretical Perspectives in Economic Geography

While most geographers would recognise and use the above concepts of space, place and scale, it is important to realise that these concepts are themselves subject to debate and alternative interpretations in geography (e.g., see Clifford et al., 2009). For example, the term space can have different meanings. Indeed, some geographers use the term space to describe *absolute* geographical space (as described above), while others are using the term to describe *relative* space or *relational* space. You need to keep this in mind when reading some geography texts. More generally, you need to be aware of the fact that economic geography is a vibrant, dynamic and continuously evolving sub-discipline composed of a diverse set of approaches and concepts. This book will help you to learn about the key approaches and concepts that contemporary economic geography has to offer. These approaches and concepts will be explained in some detail in subsequent chapters. However, already at this point, it is useful to highlight the various intellectual traditions within which these approaches and concepts are anchored. There are three main theoretical perspectives in economic geography (see also Dicken and Lloyd, 1990; Coe et al., 2007):

Neo-classical location theory
Location theory flourished in the 1950s and the 1960s and was primarily interested in establishing and explaining patterns in the distribution of economic activities across space. This type of economic geography was firmly anchored in a mainstream neo-classical economics theory with its assumption of *homo economicus*. It used a model-based approach to study the location of economic activities (e.g., firms) in space. This period in the development of economic geography is often called a 'quantitative revolution' (the emphasis was on quantitative mathematical methods in analysing spatial patterns). However, many economic geographers became dissatisfied with this approach and started exploring alternatives (see below). Despite this, quantitative approaches in geography have continued to develop and provided foundations for what is nowadays usually called 'regional science', 'geographical economics' or 'spatial economics'. More recently, the interest in regional science and

geographical economics has been further reinvigorated through the work of economist Paul Krugman and his New Economic Geography (see also below).

Structuralist approach/Marxist political economy

The political and economic turmoil of late 1960s and 1970s meant that many academics started to ask critical questions about the nature of the capitalist society and economy. A Marxist political economy approach seems to have provided many answers and since the 1970s Marxist views started to influence geographical thought – and they still have a significant influence on economic geography today. Marxist-inspired economic geography moved the attention away from spatial and locational patterns to the questions of *social relations* and power. According to Marxists, social relations of production are crucial in determining how capitalist economies work (and how they work over space). The emphasis is therefore on class relations and class struggles (between the working class and capitalists), which structure the way (capitalist) society is organised. Economic structure, in this way, determines everything else (e.g., spatial organisation of a given society simply reflects capitalist social relations). Given this position, Marxist approaches are often referred to as 'structuralist'.

Post-structuralist approaches/new economic geography/cultural turn

While Marxist ideas remain influential, since the mid-1990s, a new type of economic geography has started to emerge from 'post-structuralist' (i.e., 'post-Marxist') ideas. An important contribution of the resultant new economic geography is its insistence that economic processes cannot be seen in isolation from social, cultural and political contexts. In fact, new economic geography argues that social, cultural and/or institutional factors are central to the functioning of the economy/economies. Thus, the emphasis on the notion of class has been replaced by the interest in categories such as gender, race, age, religion and culture. This change of emphasis is often referred to as the 'cultural turn' (and is visible not only in geography, but also other social sciences). New economic geography thus stands in a stark contrast to Marxist approaches. Equally, it is important to note that this emphasis on cultural factors also represents one of the key differences between the new economic geography used by geographers and the one used by economists or spatial economists (see Box 2.1). Furthermore, the cultural turn brought with it a change of focus away from structural (general) features towards more particular (specific and place-specific) features of societies and economies. The emphasis on *place*-specific origins of cultural characteristics is, of course,

BOX 2.1   NEW ECONOMIC GEOGRAPHY

In the literature, you may come across two different versions of new economic geographies – the 'new economic geography' described by geographers and the 'New Economic Geography' (NEG) described by economists. The difference between the two reflects a fundamental difference of understanding concerning what economic geography is about. According to Paul Krugman, the key proponent of NEG, economic geography is about 'the location of production in space'; in other words, it is a 'branch of economics that worries about where things happen in relation to one another' (Krugman, 1991, p.1). In investigating the patterns of location of production in space, Krugman uses complex economic models in which geography (often simply in the form of transport costs) is inserted as an important factor. In this way, Krugman's NEG has much in common with neo-classical location theory mentioned above and further elaborated upon in Chapter 4. This book does not explore Krugman's theory in any detail (as this is beyond its scope). However, by learning about neo-classical location theory in Chapter 4 you will gain a good understanding of the basic principles on which Krugman's theory builds. This, in turn, will help you to read some of Krugman's work in the future should you choose to do so.

In contrast to NEG, the new economic geography described by geographers as part of the 'cultural turn' is not represented by one single theory. Rather it is very much a diverse set of approaches. More importantly, the new economic geography of the cultural turn represents a dramatically different view of economies and their geographies (see more in Chapter 6). While there have been attempts to foster a dialogue between geographers and economists (e.g., via the *Journal of Economic Geography* or through edited volumes such as Clark et al., 2003) the gap between the two types of new economic geographies is rather noticeable (Figure 2.3).

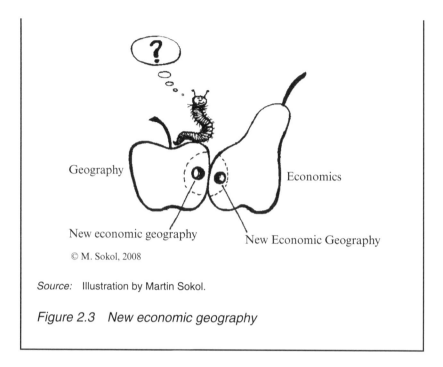

Source: Illustration by Martin Sokol.

Figure 2.3   New economic geography

of particular interest to economic geographers (and geographers more generally).

These three major theoretical perspectives will be examined step by step in the subsequent chapters of this book. Chapter 3 will highlight the key differences these perspectives (grouped under the three broad headings of neo-classical, Marxist and alternative approaches) display with regard to fundamental issues of how economies work and how economies work over space. Chapters 4, 5 and 6 will then examine each of these perspectives in detail, one by one. As will become apparent, economic geographers do not always agree which approach is the best and the concepts they are working with are continually tested and contested. None of the theoretical perspectives is perfect; each of them has its strengths and weaknesses. However, collectively, they provide critical insights into the ways in which societies and economies work (and how they work over space). The importance of economic geography for understanding the economic world around us will be explored in the subsequent section.

WHY IS ECONOMIC GEOGRAPHY IMPORTANT?

Issues for Economic Geography

The previous section highlighted the fact that economic geography can be seen as a diverse set of approaches that economic geographers use to study economic processes. On the one hand, this diversity can be seen as a weakness. On the other hand, this diversity allows economic geographers to engage with a rich and diverse set of issues related to the economy and society. Concrete questions often depend on a theoretical standpoint. Peter Dicken and Peter Lloyd, for example, offer the following definition of what economic geographers do in their influential textbook *Location in Space* (Dicken and Lloyd, 1990, p.7; original emphasis): 'Fundamentally, the economic geographer is concerned with the *spatial organisation* of economic systems: with *where* the various elements of the system are located, *how* they are connected together in space, and the *spatial impact* of economic processes'. On the basis of this, they argue that economic geographers are interested in three interconnected questions:

1. In what ways are economic activities organised spatially on the earth's surface, and how do such spatial forms or patterns change over time?
2. Why are economic activities organised spatially in particular ways; that is, what are the underlying processes at work?
3. How does the spatial organisation of economic activities itself influence economic and other social processes? (Ibid., p.8)

These are good questions, but they do not necessarily cover the whole range of other issues where economic geography can be useful. Roger Lee, for example, offers a much broader definition of what economic geography is and what economic geographers should do. In his view, economic geography is 'a geography of people's struggle to make a living' and should therefore concern itself with 'the sustainable and humane production, use and reproduction of the social, natural and material conditions of human existence' (Lee, 1994, p.147). On the basis of this, Lee (ibid., p.148) argues that an 'inclusive economic geography' should include the study of:

- the cultural and environmental origins of economic activity, articulated through socially constructed gender and kinship relations; and the struggle to establish a particular set of social relations of production and their geographical extent;

- the conceptualisation of nature;
- the forms of calculation and measurement of value;
- the processes and forms of production and consumption generated by such relations and value systems;
- the division of labour;
- the conditions of development within a particular set of social relations;
- the forms of state and politics that support and legitimise particular social relations and processes of production and consumption;
- the construction of cultural and ideological forms that shape the basis of discourse within a particular value system;
- the structuring of relationships within and between different sets of social relations;
- the conditions of transformation from one set of social relations of production to another.

This is a long list indeed – it reflects the view discussed earlier that there are 'no economies, only economic geographies' (Lee, 2006a, p.430). Put differently, given that all economic processes are inherently spatial, economic geographers should be concerned about all the processes related to the people's struggle to make a living. However, an important question arises about whether such an approach is still needed in the era of globalisation in which space is apparently being dissolved by modern information and communication technologies (ICTs).

The Age of Globalisation: The End of Geography?

Powerful arguments have been put forward about the impact of globalisation in general, and the effects of the ICT revolution in particular, on economic activities. Some observers have come to the conclusion that electronic communications have 'space-shrinking' effects and will bring about the 'death of distance' and thus, ultimately, the 'end of geography'.

The 'death of distance' thesis has been expressed by Cairncross as follows:

> Distance will no longer determine the cost of communicating electronically. Companies will organize certain types of work in three shifts according to the world's three main time zones: the Americas, East Asia/Australia, and Europe . . . No longer will location be key to most business decisions. Companies will locate any screen-based activity anywhere on earth, wherever they can find the best bargain of skills and productivity. (Cairncross, 1997, p.xi, cited in Martin, 1999a, p.15)

A similar argument has been put forward by O'Brien who argued that ICTs will allow money to be moved around the globe without constraints, thus spelling the 'end of geography':

> The end of geography, as a concept applied to international financial relationships, refers to a state of economic development where geographical location no longer matters, or matters less than hitherto. In this state, *financial market regulators* no longer hold sway over their regulatory territory; that is, rules no longer apply to specific geographical frameworks, such as the nation-state or other typical regulatory/jurisdictional territories. For *financial firms*, this means that the choice of geographical location can be greatly widened . . . *Stock exchanges* can no longer expect to monopolize trading in the shares of companies in their country or region . . . *For the consumer of financial services*, the end of geography means a wider range of services will be offered, outside the traditional services offered by local banks. (O'Brien, 1992, p.1; original emphasis; cited in Martin, 1999a, p.15)

As you can see, the authors of the above statements attempt to convince their readers that, thanks to ICTs, space and place no longer matter or at least they matter much less than before. Indeed, they both seem to suggest that location in space is no longer an issue for firms as they can locate 'anywhere on earth'. Also, the role of place is apparently greatly diminished. Cairncross, for instance, suggests that the only place characteristics that firms may be interested in can be reduced to 'the best bargain of skills and productivity'. O'Brien, in the meantime, does not seem to recognise any role that places may play in the globalised financial markets. Both statements also question the importance of scale. Indeed, both Cairncross and O'Brien seem to imply that the national scale is increasingly irrelevant in the global economy. Indeed, O'Brien specifically points out that (national) financial market regulators 'no longer hold sway' and that rules no longer apply to nation-states, because financial flows are spilling over traditional national boundaries. Similarly, Cairncross seems to suggest that the (macro-regional) time zone is the only geographical scale that holds any relevance in the new era of global electronic communications.

What is interesting about these statements of Cairncross and O'Brien is that they both see globalisation as something positive. Note, for instance, Cairncross's suggestion that companies will benefit from the new locational freedom by allowing them to find and exploit 'the best bargain of skills and productivity'. O'Brien, meanwhile, suggests that the 'end of geography' will be beneficial for both financial firms *and* their customers. Views such as these can be labelled as 'hyperglobalist' (e.g., see Held et al., 1999, pp.3–5; Dicken, 2007, pp.10–11). Some of them go as far as to suggest that freeing economic activities from their traditional geographical constraints will bring benefits to all people in all corners of the globe. However, this, manifestly, does not seem to be the case as we have seen in Chapter 1. Today's world is ridden with sharp inequalities both within and between countries and geography plays an important role in understanding economic and social processes and their uneven manifestations in the age of globalisation.

Importance of Economic Geography in the Era of Globalisation

Despite the hyperglobalist views, the role of space, place and scale does not diminish in the globalising world. Quite the opposite, perhaps. Indeed, as economic activities are increasingly internationalised, interconnections between various places increase, competition between them intensifies and, as we have seen in Chapter 1, inequalities are on the rise, so geography becomes more important than ever. In fact, as pointed out earlier, some would argue that an economic-geographical approach is perhaps 'best placed to help us appreciate and understand the modern economic world in all its complexity' (Coe et al., 2007, Preface, p.xviii). This conviction is based on the knowledge that economic geography offers powerful tools for analysing and understanding contemporary economies and societies. These tools will be introduced step by step in the chapters that follow.

As you will be able to appreciate by going through these chapters, economic geography offers some useful insights into the processes of economic globalisation. Economic geography, for example, can help us to understand why, despite years and decades of economic globalisation, the pattern of investment, production, trade and consumption is highly uneven. It can also help us to appreciate that even footloose multi-national corporations (MNCs) have to be 'grounded' in specific locations and often 'embedded' in places and their socio-political, institutional and cultural contexts. Economic geography also helps to elucidate the ways in which economic activities are 'governed' at various geographical scales from local and regional to national, macro-regional and global levels.

The economic-geographical approach can also help us to understand why, despite the widespread use of ICTs, trading places for global financial capital remain stubbornly located in a small number of global cities, which, in turn, influence economic processes around the world. Thanks to these and other insights, economic geography can thus contribute to our understanding of inequalities at various geographical scales from poverty in urban areas to global uneven development. Importantly, economic geographers also have a lot to offer in terms of understanding economic crises and the role of space in them.

CONCLUSION

This chapter introduced economic geography as a dynamic sub-discipline of geography that uses a geographical approach to study the economy. The chapter emphasised that an economic-geographical approach to studying economies is very different from the one used by mainstream economics. In highlighting these differences, the chapter introduced the key concepts of an economic-geographical approach, namely the concepts of space, place and scale. Having these and other concepts at its disposal, economic geography is uniquely placed to help us appreciate and understand the modern economic world in all its complexity. Crucially, economic geography can offer important insights into the questions of inequality and instability of the global economy. No other discipline can claim such a wide scope of interest and relevance to today's rapidly changing world. Thus, contrary to the claims of the 'end of geography', the process of globalisation is making geography more important than ever. By following the chapters of this book you will gain solid foundations in economic geography approaches, concepts and theories and their applicability to the contemporary world. It is important to note, however, that economic geography is not a unified body of theory. Rather, various diverse, and often conflicting, approaches are present within economic geography. The following chapter will provide an introduction to the three main theoretical perspectives – neo-classical, Marxist and alternative perspectives. The chapter will highlight the way in which these three perspectives differ on fundamental questions such as how economies work and how economies work over space.

FURTHER READING

Coe, N.M., P.F. Kelly and H.W.C. Yeung (2007) *Economic Geography: A Contemporary Introduction.* (Oxford: Blackwell) Chapter 1.
Dicken, P. (2011) *Global Shift: Mapping the Changing Contours of the World Economy (Sixth edition).* (London: Sage) Chapters 1 and 2.
MacKinnon, D. and A. Cumbers (2007) *An Introduction to Economic Geography: Globalization, Uneven Development and Place.* (Harlow: Pearson/Prentice Hall) Chapter 1.
Pike, A., A. Rodriguez-Pose and J. Tomaney (2006) *Local and Regional Development.* (London and New York: Routledge) Chapter 1.

USEFUL WEBSITES*

http://geog.uconn.edu/aag-econ/ – website of the Economic Geography Specialty Group of the Association of American Geographers (AAG).

http://www.egrg.org.uk/ – website of the Economic Geography Research Group (EGRG) of the Royal Geographical Society-Institute of British Geographers (RGS-IBG).

* Both accessed 26 February 2011.

3. Key approaches in economic geography

INTRODUCTION

The previous chapter introduced economic geography as a sub-discipline of geography that uses a geographical approach to study economies. It highlighted the fact that the economic-geographical approach of studying economies is very different from the one used by mainstream economics. The chapter noted that economic geographers study the economy using the concepts of space, place and scale.

What the chapter has *not* done is to explore the question of what 'the economy' actually is. This is, however, a fundamental question. Indeed, the way in which we define what the economy is influences our understanding of how the economy works and what can be done about it. Importantly, the definition of the economy and 'the economic' also has an important bearing on our understanding of the way economic processes work over space, across scales and in particular places. In other words, the way in which we define the economy has profound implications for our understanding of economic geographies.

This chapter thus aims to address this issue by exploring the different theoretical perspectives on the economy and their geographical implications. The point here is not to provide a detailed description of the various economic geography concepts as this will be provided in subsequent chapters. Rather the aim here is to allow the reader to grasp and recognise the key differences in the theoretical foundations on which various economic geography concepts have been developed. As already noted in the previous chapter, economic geography is not a monolithic sub-discipline. Indeed, Chapter 2 introduced three main theoretical perspectives. These will be further explored in the present chapter under the following headings:

- the mainstream economic perspective (i.e., perspective based on neo-classical economics);
- the Marxist approach (i.e., structuralist political economy perspective);

- alternative approaches (including evolutionary-institutional approach).

As will become apparent through this chapter, these three perspectives represent contrasting views on how the economy works and in turn offer three quite different ways of approaching economic geographies. But first, let us explore the question of what the economy is.

WHAT IS THE ECONOMY?

Defining the Economy

Let us start with a definition of 'the economy'. The term is used in everyday life with such frequency that we rarely pause to think what the economy actually is. Most people take the notion of the economy for granted. In fact, many economics dictionaries and textbooks take it for granted too and do not even bother defining it (for example, see *The Penguin Dictionary of Economics* by Bannock et al., 1998, or *A Dictionary of Economics* by Black, 2002). The term 'economy' did not feature in the original version of Raymond Williams' (1976) *Keywords* either.

So what is the economy? *The Concise Oxford English Dictionary* (Soanes and Stevenson, 2006) suggests that the word 'economy' is in fact of Greek origin. The Greek term *oikonomia* basically means 'household management' – from *oikos* 'house' and *nomos* 'managing' from *nemein* 'manage' (see also *Online Etymology Dictionary* by Harper, 2001). The hint of this original meaning still survives today and economy can mean 'careful management of available resources'. In travel, for example, this can mean that you buy the cheapest air or rail ticket and travel 'economy class' (see Soanes and Stevenson, 2006).

However, since about the eighteenth century the term economy also began to gain a new meaning and now can refer to economic affairs at a much larger geographical scale, namely that of a nation (see Coe et al., 2007, p.38). Indeed, even nowadays, the notion of the economy is perhaps still most commonly used to describe the economic processes of a nation or country (although it is increasingly being used in connection with other geographical scales, e.g., the 'local economy', the 'European economy' or the 'global economy'). *The Concise Oxford English Dictionary* defines the economy as 'the state of a country or area in terms of the production and consumption of goods and services and the supply of money' (Soanes and Stevenson, 2006). However, as will become apparent below, even this latter (and commonly accepted) definition is in fact somewhat problematic.

Measuring the Economy

Perhaps the most common way of measuring 'the state in which a country is in terms of the production and consumption of goods and services' is an indicator called *gross domestic product* (GDP) and we have come across it in Chapter 1. GDP measures, in money terms, the total market value of production in a particular economy in a given year. It is usually calculated as a sum of expenditures by households, firms and the government plus net exports. By *household expenditure* (or *consumption expenditure*) we mean the total amount spent by individuals in a given year including their expenditure on food, fuel, housing, clothing, household appliances, leisure, and so on. Expenditure by firms is measured as *investment expenditure*, by which we mean the amount invested by businesses in future productive capacity. *Government expenditure* is the amount spent by the government to build infrastructure (e.g., roads or railways) or provide services (e.g., health or education). Finally, *net exports* represent the value of goods and services sold to other countries minus the value of goods and services imported from abroad (see Coe et al., 2007, p.34, Figure 2.2).

Problematising and Re-defining the Economy

GDP represents a fairly standard way of measuring the economy. It captures three key economic agents – namely households, firms and the government – all of which play important roles in the economy. Yet measuring the economy in this way can be highly problematic. One of the key problems is that GDP measurement is derived from a definition of the economy that is rather narrow – it includes certain things and processes but excludes others. Coe et al. (2007, p.35) offer a very good example of this problem. If you have taken a bus or drive a car to your place of work or study then you have engaged in an economic act. Your bus fare or your fuel bills and parking costs would be included in your individual consumption and therefore included in the conventional definition of the economy. But if you decide to cycle or walk instead, no money will change hands and, therefore, oddly, you have not engaged in an economic act! Another good example is unpaid work (e.g., cooking at home, or bringing up children). Since no wages are paid, unpaid work occurs outside the formal monetary economy and therefore is not included in the consideration of the state of the economy. This way, not only is the economy *mis*counted, but also the work of certain people is *dis*counted (ibid., p.45). Clearly, we have a problem here.

A similar problem arises with the informal or semi-informal economy (sometimes also called 'black economy' or 'grey economy'). In the informal or semi-informal economy, money can in fact change hands, but because these monetary transactions are not recorded by the government, they are not included in what counts as 'the economy'. Yet, the livelihoods of millions of people around the world may be dependent on such transactions. Thinking about what constitutes an economic act or process is crucial for our understanding of the economy and is, therefore, a point of contention.

The way in which cultural, social, political and environmental processes are related to the economic processes is another contentious issue. A conventional definition of the economy (which places rigid boundaries around the 'economic') supports the impression that the economy is somewhat separated from other dimensions of our lives. This in turn helps to create the impression that the economy is something 'out there', which affects our lives, but which we, as individuals, cannot control. This impression is often reinforced by the way the economy is represented in everyday use and policy documents. Indeed, the economy is often represented by metaphors such as a 'machine', an 'organism' or a 'body'; that presumably has a life of its own and 'outside of any kind of collective control – that is, it is something that controls *us* rather than the other way around' (ibid., p.36; original emphasis). However, it could be argued that the economy is inseparable from cultural, social, political and environmental processes. This also means that the process of economic globalisation is inseparable from other dimensions of globalisation, be it social, political or cultural (e.g., see Jones, 2006, p.113). This also has important implications for the definition of the economy. Ray Hudson, for instance, understands the economy as referring to 'those simultaneously discursive and material processes and practices of production, distribution and consumption, through which people seek to create wealth, prosperity and well-being and so construct economies; to circuits of production, circulation, realisation, appropriation and distribution of value' (Hudson, 2005, p.1). This is rather a mouthful, but it is important to note that Hudson is talking about *value* rather than money or GDP. And he is quick to add that value is '*always* culturally constituted and defined' (ibid.; original emphasis) and that '[w]hat counts as "the economy" is, therefore, always cultural, constituted in and distributed over space, linked by flows of values, monies, things and people that conjoin a diverse heterogeneity of people and things' (ibid., pp.1–2). He further argues that '[e]qually importantly, the social processes that constitute the economy *always* involve biological, chemical or physical transformation via human labour of elements of the natural world' (ibid., p.2; original emphasis).

This also means that thinking about the economy in terms of ever-growing GDP, for instance, may not be a universally shared, nor necessarily desirable, concept. Indeed, as Hodder and Lee (1974, p.7) have argued several decades ago, it is 'all too easy, for instance, to assume that the dream of each less-developed country is to become developed', and, 'such a view can easily disregard highly developed local cultures' (ibid.). Hodder and Lee add that 'self-respect is at least as important a measure of social and economic progress as are increases in . . . material wealth' (ibid.). Similarly, studying the economy without considering the environmental dimension of economic processes is flawed, not least because 'economic activities are taking an increasing toll of balanced interactions within the life-giving eco-system' (ibid., p.9). The Western obsession with GDP and GDP growth is therefore hugely problematic (see also discussion in Chapter 8).

Another way to approach a definition of the economy is to remind ourselves of the notion introduced in Chapter 2 that there are 'no econo-mies, only economic geographies' (Lee, 2006a, p.430). In turn, economic geographies can be defined as 'geographies of people's struggle to make a living' (Lee, 1994, p.147) (see Chapter 2). Importantly, this strug-gle to make a living is framed in both material and social processes. In other words, 'all economies and economic geographies are both material *and* social constructs' (Leyshon and Lee, 2003, p.8; original emphasis). What is more, in the construction of economic geographies the relations between the material and the social are 'inseparable and mutually forma-tive' (ibid.). The recognition of this further undermines the notion of the economy as simply being 'the state of production and consumption of goods and service and the supply of money' or as being measurable by GDP and forces us to think more carefully about what the economy is (see also Gibson-Graham, 2005 for a critique).

HOW DOES THE ECONOMY WORK?

The previous section has highlighted the fact that answering the question 'What is the economy?' is not straightforward. The process of defining the economy can be problematic and what should (or should not) be included in the notion of the economy remains a contentious issue. This section will attempt to address an issue that is even more contentious: 'How does the economy work?' As already pointed out in the opening paragraphs of this chapter, the answer to this question is in part influenced by the way we define the economy. However, even people who would share the view about what the economy *is* can disagree profoundly on the question of how it *works*. Large numbers of economists and social scientists around the world are trying to understand how economies work and there is no space here to review all of their theories. Instead, this section will identify the main features of the three key theoretical perspectives on the economy.

First, the section will examine the mainstream economic perspective, which sees the functioning of the economy through the lens of market forces and which maintains that individual self-interest mediated by the 'invisible hand' of the market leads to equilibrium and prosperity. Second, the section will introduce the Marxist perspective, which, in contrast, argues that the capitalist market economy is ridden by internal contradictions and produces both inequality and instability. Finally, we will have a look at the alternative approaches, especially those associated with evolutionary and institutionalist economics, which try to go beyond the boundaries of market-based processes and which pay attention to wider social, cultural and institutional contexts in order to explain how economies function.

Mainstream Economic Perspective

The mainstream economic perspective is mainly associated with *neo-classical economic theory*, which currently represents the dominant way of looking at the economy. Neo-classical economics is rooted in the belief that the market is the most efficient mechanism for the allocation of resources and hence the creation of prosperity. The neo-classical school of economic thought has been built on the foundations laid down by Adam Smith, a Scottish economist and the founder of the *classical political economy*. Back in the eighteenth century, Smith devised an economic theory, the features of which remain with us today. These include his concepts of rational self-interest and the 'invisible hand' of the market, concepts that underpin much of contemporary mainstream economic thinking.

In seeking to identify how wealth is created, Adam Smith argued that the main cause of prosperity is the *division of labour*. Smith expressed his arguments in his famous work titled *An Inquiry into the Nature and Causes of the Wealth of Nations* published in 1776. In it, Smith used an example of a factory making pins to explain the power of the division of labour and the productivity that can be achieved from this (Figure 3.1). He argued that a single worker working alone at home would be lucky to produce even one pin per day and certainly not 20. However, he observed that in a pin-making factory ten workers can engage in the production of pins by dividing 18 specialised pin-making tasks between them (Figure 3.1):

> One man draws out the wire, another straights it, a third cuts it, a fourth points it, a fifth grinds it at the top for receiving the head; to make the head requires two or three distinct operations; to put it on, is a peculiar business, to whiten the pins is another; it is even a trade by itself to put them into the paper; and the important business of making a pin is, in this manner, divided into about eighteen distinct operations, which, in some manufactories, are all performed by distinct hands, though in others the same man will sometimes perform two or three of them. (Smith, 1776, I.1.3)

Source: www.timesonline.co.uk/tol/news/uk/article617514.ece.

*Figure 3.1   Division of labour in a pin-making factory described by Adam
            Smith in his* An Inquiry into the Nature and Causes of the
            Wealth of Nations

By dividing the work between them in this way, Smith argued, ten
workers can together produce about 48,000 pins per day. That is 4,800
pins per worker per day, representing a massive improvement of productivity when compared with the output achievable without the division of
labour.

The above improvement of productivity in the pin-making factory is
impressive indeed. But how does the pin-making factory know how many
pins to produce and at what price to sell them? According to mainstream
economists, this problem will be solved by what Smith called the 'invisible
hand' of the market. The market will determine both the quantity of goods
produced and the price at which these goods will be sold, by matching
supply with *demand*. This is how it works (see Figure 3.2). From a producer's point of view, the higher the price customers are prepared to pay for a
product (i.e., a pin) the more the producer will be prepared to produce. This
is represented by the upward-sloping *supply curve* in Figure 3.2. However,
the higher the price, the less the goods will be in demand by the customers –
shown as the downward-sloping *demand curve* in Figure 3.2. Under perfect
market conditions, supply and demand curves will intersect in the middle,
thus fixing both the quantity of goods to be produced and the price under
which they will be sold. In other words, the markets will achieve *equilibrium*
(see Figure 3.2; see also Dicken and Lloyd, 1990, pp.5–6).

However, the functioning of the economy in the way described above,
is based on the expectation that both producers and consumers are acting
in a rational, economising or profit-maximising way. In other words, they
are behaving as *homo economicus*, a notion we have introduced in Chapter

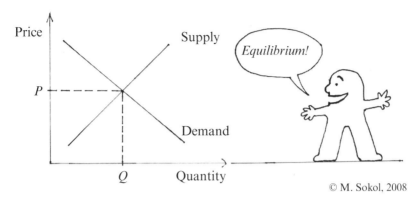

Source: Adapted from Dicken and Lloyd (1990, Figure I.1, p.5).

Figure 3.2   Market economy: the equilibrium relationship of demand, supply and price

2. Adam Smith argued that such behaviour is motivated by 'self-interest'. He further argued that *by pursuing their own self-interests, individuals, led by the 'invisible hand' of the market, are unintentionally contributing to a greater societal good, a win–win situation, from which everybody will benefit*. If pin-makers, shoe-makers, butchers and bakers all pursue their individual self-interest, the market will ensure that everybody will be better off.

Since the times of Adam Smith, economic theory has developed a lot, but the key principles he introduced are still with us. The analysis of the workings of the economy through the lens of rational profit-making agents (individuals or firms) and the belief that markets are capable of delivering both equilibrium and efficiency, is central to neo-classical economic theory (and to mainstream economics more generally). Indeed, as we shall see in Chapter 8, some economists argue that economic crises happen due to interference with market forces (e.g., over-regulation) and that they can be resolved by letting the 'invisible hand' of the market do its work. However, such an understanding of the economy and the crises has been challenged by the Marxist approach, which will be examined in turn.

The Marxist Approach

The Marxist perspective on the economy is derived from the work of Karl Marx and Friedrich Engels, two German philosophers of the late nineteenth century. Like Adam Smith, Karl Marx was interested in the question of how wealth is created in the economy and how wealth is distributed among members of society. However, in stark contrast to the win–win situation alluded to by Smith, Marx pointed out that wealth will increasingly concentrate in the hands of the few. How so? To answer this question, Marx devised his *labour theory of value*.

In order to explain the basics of the labour theory of value as devised by Marx, let us go back to the pin-making factory described earlier. As we have seen, the productivity gains from organising pin production in the pin factory were substantial. But who reaps the benefits? If the factory was jointly owned by the ten workers who work there, it is possible to imagine a situation in which they could split the benefits of their production between themselves. However, in the capitalist market economy, the factory is likely to be privately owned. The owner, the capitalist, would own the land on which the factory is built, the factory building itself, the raw materials needed to produce the pins and all the machinery and tools used by the workers. In other words, he or she would own the *means of production*. Workers, on the other hand, do not possess the means of production and the only way they can sustain themselves is to sell their own work (or as Marxists call it, their *labour power*) to capitalists. Thus, in the capitalist market economy, labour itself becomes a commodity – labour power can be bought and sold like any other commodity. So, workers sell their labour and receive wages in exchange for their work and that looks fine on the surface.

However, the question arises as to what capitalists do to sustain themselves? They have to engage in the circuit of capital and make *profit*. The way Marx described how the circuit of capital works is presented in Figure 3.3. Imagine a capitalist who has capital in the form of money – *money capital* (M) – to invest. He or she can turn this money capital into *productive capital* (P) by purchasing two commodities – the *labour power* (LP; e.g., labour of ten workers) and the *means of production* (MP; e.g., pin-making factory, raw materials, machinery, tools, etc., needed to produce pins). The labour power and the means of production are then combined in the process of production to produce 48,000 pins a day – representing another form of capital – *commodity capital* (C). Commodity capital can be turned back into money capital when the factory owner sells pins on the market at a certain price (and this price represents what Marxists call *exchange value*). For the capitalist to survive, he or she has to make a profit. This means that the money he or she receives in exchange for the commodities produced must be greater than the money originally invested in the enterprise ($M' > M$). The search for profit is the motivating force of the capitalist economy.

The crucial point in the Marxist analysis is a suggestion that, ultimately,

© M. Sokol, 2008

Note: M = money capital, C = commodity capital, LP = labour power, MP = means of production, P = production process, C' = increased commodity capital, s = surplus value, M' = increased money capital.

Source: Adapted from Hudson (2005, p.26, Figure 2.2); Lee (2006b, p.22, Figure 3); Dicken and Lloyd (1990, p.356, Figure 9.5).

Figure 3.3 Circuit of capital in the capitalist economy

all value comes from human labour and the only way for a capitalist to make profit is to appropriate *surplus value* (the little '*s*'). Surplus value is the difference between the wages the factory owner pays workers for their labour and the value these workers produce for him or her in the factory while making pins. To frame it differently, workers add value to the commodities they produce by applying their labour, and this value is greater than the reward they get in exchange for their efforts in the form of wages. This is the basis of *exploitation* in the capitalist economy. However, capitalists have to engage in it, if they are to survive the cut-throat competition from other capitalists, who have to do exactly the same. Those capitalists who fail to generate profit (or enough profit) go out of business. The effort to maximise profit is therefore an imperative of the capitalist economy. All capitalists, individually, have to act in a profit-maximising manner, which echoes the self-interested behaviour described by Adam Smith. Such behaviour, in turn, further exacerbates competition and so it could be argued that one of the key features of capitalism is that it is inherently competitive.

However, Marx argued that such individual action will not lead to the equilibrium and win–win situation envisaged by Smith – far from it. Marx argued that capitalism (the system based on capital) is both unequal and unstable. He argued that inequalities within society will *increase* as capitalists try to increase their profits and squeeze workers' wages, by introducing machines, intensifying labour processes or simply by forcing workers to work longer hours, for example. Capitalists can also endeavour to replace workers by machines and by doing so, they create a growing pool of the unemployed, which in turn will push wages down further still. The result of this process will be an increasing concentration of wealth in the hands of a few (the capitalist class) and the impoverishment of the working class masses (proletariat). Simply put, the capitalist system will ensure that the rich will become richer and the poor will become poorer.

Ethical issues aside, Marx argued that such a system is unlikely to reach an equilibrium of the kind envisaged by Adam Smith, because sooner or later the fundamental economic *contradiction* arises: too many commodities (e.g., pins) will be produced, but there will be too few people able to buy them. Marxists call this situation an *overaccumulation*. Overaccumulation can take various forms, but overaccumulation of capital in the form of unsold commodities is one of the most striking symptoms. The most recent economic crisis has offered a stark reminder of this. Among the most iconic and most visible examples have been growing inventories of unsold cars piling up at manufacturers' car parks around the world, causing grave difficulties to the industry. Ian Craib offers a very good illustration of how such a crisis of overaccumulation can happen, using a crucial distinction in Marxist theory between *use value* and *exchange value*:

> If I am a worker and I produce £50 worth of goods in a day (the use value of my labour to my employer), and I receive £10 a day in wages (the exchange value of my labour power), then I do not receive in wages sufficient [amount] to buy back the value of goods I have produced. This applies right across the system, so that if stocks of unsold goods build up, workers have to be laid off, and the economy enters a crisis, a depression, or slump, until the stock of goods are used up and firms go back into production. There is a cycle of growth and slump, something that capitalist economies have been trying to deal with for over a century and a half. (Craib, 1997, pp.94–5)

This is then one of the possible causes of the familiar boom-and-bust cycle (see more in Wolff and Resnick, 1987, pp.185–92; Shaik, 1991). Each boom is followed by a crisis in which *devaluation* must take place to kick-start the accumulation process all over again. For Marx then, *the capitalist economy is neither equal nor stable – it is inherently unequal and crisis-prone*. The profit-making imperative that drives the capitalist economy and makes it dynamic is also a source of its fundamental contradiction. Marxist conceptualisation of the economy therefore represents a stark contrast to the equilibrium-prone and win–win expectations of mainstream economics. And it is important to note that *the instability of the capitalist economy is directly linked to the inequality it produces*. Indeed,

Marxist economists argue that it is the inequality in society that is the root of the recent global financial and economic crisis (see Chapter 8 for a discussion).

Importantly, Marx also argued that in the long run the capitalist system is unsustainable, because the increasing contradictions will reach a tipping point at which the system will eventually collapse. This, according to Marx, will happen in the most advanced capitalist countries, where the contradictions between labour and capital will be the greatest. The collapse of capitalism will pave a way (via a socialist revolution led by the working class) for a new social and economic order (communism). Marx said very little about how such a new system would operate. However, for a system to be freed from exploitation, both private property and class relations based on property rights would probably have to be abolished. Indeed, it is the ownership of the means of production (and *social relations* of production that it creates) that is the source of considerable power and while this source of power continues to exist, it is, for Marxists, hard to consider a market economy as 'fair'.

While Marxism provides a powerful analysis of the way the economy works, it also leaves us with a number of important issues. Indeed, the economy does not always work as predicted by Marx and, so far, the socialist revolution has failed to materialise in the most advanced capitalist countries. One of the key questions therefore is how can we account for the fact that the capitalist system manages to survive despite its contradictions? As we shall see below, economic geographers have made an important contribution to the debate on this question. But for now, let's turn to the alternative approaches.

Alternative Approaches

It is clear from the above examination of the mainstream economic and Marxist perspectives that they differ dramatically in their analysis of the workings of the economy. However, despite the differences, these two perspectives also share one common feature – they both focus on formal market transactions. Indeed, as we have seen, mainstream economics is concerned with the relationship between the demand and supply of goods or services as expressed by a price fixed through the market mechanism. The Marxist analysis, meanwhile, focuses on the (hidden) difference between the price of labour (exchange value of labour power) and the exchange value of the commodities produced by the labour. However, as we have seen in the opening section of this chapter, what constitutes 'the economy' and 'the economic' is a contentious issue. Echoing these concerns, a number of alternative economic approaches have emerged. These approaches usually fall within a category of *heterodox economics* since they are providing a counterbalance to the established mainstream (ortho-dox) economic views. One of the leading heterodox approaches is associ-ated with evolutionary and institutional economics (e.g., Williamson, 1975; Nelson and Winter, 1982; Hodgson, 1988, 1993, 1998).

Evolutionary and institutional economics is in itself a diverse set of approaches, but there are some key shared characteristics that clearly distinguish these approaches from both the mainstream economics and Marxist perspectives. The starting point of evolutionary-institutional and other alternative approaches is their insistence that the economy cannot be reduced to market transactions only. Instead, they argue that wider social, cultural and institutional contexts need to be taken into consideration if one is to explain how economies work. Institutional contexts are defined broadly here and may include both formal institutions (e.g., laws, regula-tions, formal procedures) and informal institutions (e.g., habits, customs, conventions, cultural norms, etc.) at various scales – from the level of the firm to the institutional landscapes underpinning the whole economy.

The inclusion of the wider social, cultural and institutional consid-erations has profound implications for the understanding of the ways economies work. Importantly, such an inclusion challenges the neo-classical notion of the rational behaviour of 'economic man' guided by the 'invisible hand' of the market. Instead, *evolutionary and institutional economics emphasises the way in which social institutions play an essential role in guiding the action of economic agents.* (This also differs from the Marxist view that the role of economic agents is *structured* by the prevail-ing social relations of production.) In the evolutionary-institutionalist view, firms, for instance, are not seen as atomistic units competing against each other on the free market. Rather, firms are perceived as being *embed-ded* within wider socioeconomic relations and networks. These networks may include various formal and informal links with suppliers, customers and competitors. Importantly, transactions within these networks are not simply guided by market competition. Rather they often involve valuable elements of *coordination* and *cooperation*. This is important because such cooperative networks are often crucial for fostering *innovation*, which is seen as vital for economic development or economic *evolution*. In turn, this raises the question whether the 'pure market' is the best mechanism for ensuring economic progress. Evolutionary and institutionalist economists would argue that successful economies are neither pure markets nor pure hierarchies. Instead, successful economies are *mixed economies* (e.g., see Lundvall and Johnson, 1994) with important roles for the public sector and for different kinds of policy. Mixed economic systems are also seen as capable of producing a diversity of economic forms, which contributes to the adaptability and long-term survival of economic systems (rather than just the simple short-term 'survival of the fittest' enforced by unfettered markets).

Another line of argument advanced by alternative approaches relates to the claim that successful economies are increasingly knowledge-intensive or knowledge-based. The *knowledge-based economy* can be simply defined as an economy in which knowledge becomes the key economic resource. While all economies can be seen as knowledge-based, there is a perception that we witness a major shift in the relative importance of land, physical capital and knowledge capital, in favour of the latter. For some observers, the shift towards the knowledge-based economy represents an epochal transformation. As Burton-Jones (1999, p.3) vividly put it:

> Since ancient times, wealth and power have been associated with the owner-ship of physical resources. The traditional factors of production, materials, labour, and money, have been largely physical in nature. Historically the need for knowledge has been limited, and access to it largely controlled by those owning the means of production. Steam power, physical labour, and money capital largely facilitated the Industrial Revolution . . . In contrast, future wealth and power will be derived mainly from intangible, intellectual resources: knowledge capital. This transformation from a world largely dominated by physical resources, to a world dominated by knowledge, implies a shift in the locus of economic power as profound as that which occurred at the time of the Industrial Revolution. We are in the early stages of a 'Knowledge Revolution'.

The notion that the economy is moving towards a post-industrial, knowledge-intensive phase, in turn, opens up a whole set of questions. Both mainstream (neo-classical) economics and Marxist approaches have been devised in the context of an (emerging) industrial era. But will the same principles apply to the new knowledge economy?

Evolutionary and institutionalist economists have devised their own approaches to account for the ways knowledge economies work. One of the most influential concepts is that of the *learning economy* introduced by Lundvall and Johnson (1994). The starting point of the learning economy concept is the argument that if knowledge is the most fundamental resource in our contemporary economy, then learning is 'the most impor-tant process' (Lundvall and Johnson, 1994, p.23). Although Lundvall and Johnson admit that knowledge always has been a 'crucial resource' for the economy, and was in the past 'layered in traditions and routines', they argue that knowledge and learning have more recently become much more fundamental resources than before (ibid., p.24). They argue that the economy is now characterised by 'new constellations of knowledge and learning in the economy' (ibid.) mainly through the development of ICTs, flexible specialisation and, finally, changes in the process of innovation (ibid., pp.24–5). These changes are bringing challenges that firms have responded to by changing organisational forms and by building alliances in order to gain access to a more diversified knowledge base (ibid., p.25). This implies 'broader participation in learning processes' to include all layers within the firm, the development of 'multi-skilling and networking skills' and enhancing the 'capacity to learn and to apply learning to the processes of production and sales' (ibid., pp.25–6). This is why Lundvall and Johnson 'regard . . . capitalist economies not only as knowledge-based economies but also as "learning economies"' (ibid., p.26). They offer the following definition of the learning economy:

> The learning economy is a dynamic concept; it involves the capacity to learn and to expand the knowledge base. It refers not only to the importance of the science and technology systems – universities, research organisations, in-house R&D departments and so on – but also to the learning implications of the economic structure, the organisational forms and the institutional set-up. (Ibid.)

At the core of the learning economy are apparently firms that 'start to learn how to learn' (ibid.) and which are able to handle various types of knowledge. Lundvall and Johnson distinguish at least four categories of knowledge: *know-what, know-why, know-who* (when and where) and *know-how* (ibid., p.27). The first category, know-what, represents knowledge about 'facts'. The meaning of this is probably close to that of 'information'. The, second category, know-why, refers to scientific knowledge of principles and laws of motion in nature and in society. This kind of knowledge, Lundvall and Johnson argue, is extremely important for technological development (ibid.). The third term, know-who (together with know-when and know-where) is already a more complex construction that reaches a sphere of specific social relations and time–space dimension. A simple example of know-who can be a situation when, for a successful innovation, it is more important to know key persons than to know basic scientific principles (ibid., p.28). Know-when and know-where refer to economically useful knowledge about markets with their temporal and spatial dimensions, for instance. Finally, know-how refers to practical skills in production or other spheres of economic activity (ibid.).

Lundvall and Johnson (1994) also address different aspects of learning. Importantly, they do not understand learning as a simple absorption of science and technical knowledge. Rather, they define it more broadly as learning (about) changes in economic structures, organisational and institutional forms. Learning is presented as a dynamic and interactive process aimed at the accumulation of knowledge at the level of the firm and the economy as a whole. Learning is present in both production and consumption processes and is expressed through 'learning by doing' and 'learning by using'. From the point of view of permanent renewal (learning) and adaptation of economic and organisational structures, Lundvall and Johnson have also introduced an innovative term *forgetting* (ibid., p.40). They argue that the learning economy should not only preserve and store its pool of knowledge, but also should be able to 'forget'. Forgetting at the level of individual workers refers to their ability to abandon obsolete skills and professional expertise. An example of forgetting at the level of the firm or economy includes closing down ailing branches or whole sectors. Thus, the learning economy is supposed to intelligently manage continuous self-organised learning (and forgetting). As we shall see below, the work of Lundvall and Johnson and other evolutionary-institutionalists has proved highly influential in framing the discussion on contemporary economic geographies, despite the fact that there remain questions about the precise nature of the supposed transformation of the economy towards the knowledge-based economy or learning economy (e.g., see Sokol, 2004).

One contentious issue relates to the question of whether the transformation beyond an old industrial economy also signifies a move beyond a capitalist economy. Geoffrey Hodgson – one of the prominent evolutionary-institutionalist economists – contributed to the debate by offering his own definitions of the knowledge-intensive economy and learning economy. Hodgson has argued that the knowledge-intensive economy would still be a capitalist one (see Hodgson, 1999, pp.214–15), but it would be an economy in which an 'enlightened group of business leaders' is 'aware of the kind of democratic culture and participatory industrial relations that facilitate productivity'. Alongside 'collaborative and co-operative relationships between firms . . . against the neo-liberal insistence on fierce, price-driven, market competition' (ibid., p.211), Hodgson suggests that: '[s]uch a progressive movement of business people could find valuable allies among trade unionists and the population as a whole' (ibid.). However, for Hodgson, the learning economy or 'market cognitism' (ibid., p.213), in contrast, is a scenario clearly 'beyond capitalism' (ibid., pp.211–15) where the 'degree of control by the employer over the employee is minimal' (ibid., p.212). Hodgson has argued that such an economy, 'would not be socialist, in any common sense of the word', but nevertheless, 'it is not capitalism' (ibid., p.213) presumably because the means of production (brains of knowledge workers) are effectively controlled by the workers themselves, not by the employers (capitalists). Such a benign view of the emerging new 'knowledge era' thus implies that the contradictions identified by Marx as inherent to the capitalist economy may be waning. This point is hotly debated, however (e.g., see May, 2002). Regardless, evolutionary-institutionalist views in general, and knowledge-based approaches in particular, have had significant influence on the debate about economic development in the global era. Indeed, many believe that we now live in some sort of global knowledge economy (e.g., Archibugi et al., 1999) or global information society (e.g., Castells, 2000). Equally, evolutionary-institutionalist views have shaped the conceptualisation of economic geographies of this supposedly new, global, knowledge-driven era (see below).

HOW DOES THE ECONOMY WORK OVER SPACE?

Introduction

The perspectives on the economy presented above offer a good starting point to explore the question of what the economy is and how it works. However, the problem is that all views presented above could be seen as 'aspatial' – that is, they do not tell us much about how economies work over space. Yet, as already mentioned in Chapter 2, all economies must 'take place'. Economic and geographical considerations are, in other words, impossible to separate. The question of how the economy (or economies) work(s) over space, across scales and in particular places, is the key question of economic geography.

This is an important question, because as already highlighted in Chapter 1 (and as will become clear from the remaining chapters of this book), economic processes are enfolding in space in a highly uneven way and are engaged in producing and reproducing inequalities at various spatial scales. How can we explain this uneven and unequal development? The three perspectives on the economy presented in the previous section provide three very different (in fact, contrasting) ways of approaching this question. In other words, different perspectives on the economy have profound implications for the theoretical conceptualisation of economic geographies.

Neo-classical Approach, Location Theory and Beyond

Let us start with the neo-classical approach. The application of the neo-classical model for the understanding of the ways in which the economy works over space looks straightforward enough. Echoing the view that the 'invisible hand' of the market will ensure equilibrium between demand and supply, neo-classical theory of spatial development implies that any uneven development is temporary, because market forces will ensure that some sort of *spatial equilibrium* or balanced development will be achieved in the long run. This view is based on the assumption that, following the logic of the rational *economic man*, both producers (firms) and consumers (workers) will move between regions in search of the most profitable location. Simply put, labour will move from poorer to richer regions (in search of higher wages) and capital will move in the opposite direction (in search of cheaper labour and land).

Even more complex neo-classical models that involve other factors of production (e.g., technology) are all *built around the assumption that some sort of spatial equilibrium will be achieved in the long run*, because such factors of production will inevitably *spread* or *disperse* over space. Indeed, based on this assumption, globalisation enthusiasts would argue that economic globalisation would benefit all corners of the world. The processes of *spatial dispersal* can indeed be observed in reality and some countries (e.g., India and China) may have benefited from a relocation of industries from high-income countries (see also Chapter 7). However, the examples of *spatial equilibrium* that the neo-classical theory envisages, are hard to find, even within individual countries.

One way of accounting for this discrepancy is to acknowledge that, in real life, factors of production cannot move 'freely' over space. Indeed, there are various constraints involved. One of the obvious obstacles is the *friction of distance*. In other words, geography clearly plays a role. The calculation of the cost associated with moving people, machinery, materials or goods across space and the implication of this for location in space forms the basis of the *neo-classical location theory*. Key concepts that build upon the location theory include the *central place theory*, *urban hierarchy*, *market potential* and *accessibility*, all of which will be explored in more detail in Chapter 4. These concepts help us to understand how the friction of distance influences the location of economic activities in space.

Further insights into why economic activities simply do not disperse in space are, among others, offered by the concepts of *agglomeration economies*, *increasing returns* and *cumulative causation*. These latter concepts identify additional market advantages arising from the spatial *concentration* of economic activities (see more in Chapter 4). In essence, these concepts show that *rather than having a self-correcting dispersal effect, market forces can in fact reinforce existing inequalities in space*. The kind of spatial equilibrium envisaged by the neo-classical theory is therefore hard to achieve (see more in Chapter 4). It could be argued that these latter concepts 'use the approach and language of neo-classical economics to reach contrary conclusions' (Pike et al., 2006, p.70). Some of the work of the New Economic Geography à la Krugman (see Box 2.1 in Chapter 2) falls within this category.

Marxist-inspired Approaches and Uneven Development

Marxist-inspired approaches in economic geography also challenge the neo-classical idea of spatial equilibrium, although coming from a completely different perspective. As we have seen earlier in this chapter, Marxist theory sees capitalism as a system based on the exploitation of labour. The profit imperative makes such a system incredibly dynamic, yet, at the same time, inherently unequal and crisis-prone. Internal contradictions mean that crises of overaccumulation are inevitable in such a system. Devaluation must take place to kick-start the accumulation process all over again. Building on these systemic features of capitalism, Marxist economic geographers do not foresee inequalities in space disappearing with the operation of market forces. Instead they consider *uneven development as a permanent, unavoidable and, in fact, necessary feature of the capitalist market economy*. Indeed, in Marxist-inspired approaches, uneven development is usually seen as both the necessary precondition and the unavoidable consequence of capitalist economic growth.

Several concepts have been put forward that try to describe the way capitalist economies work over space (and these will be examined in detail in Chapter 5). One of these concepts uses a 'see-saw' metaphor to describe the ebb and flow of capital from one region to another in search of profit (see Smith, 1984). Destruction and devaluation of places left behind may create preconditions for future renewed growth. In a similar vein, the concept of *spatial fix* recognises that geographical space is an important element in the functioning of the capitalist economy and its ability to contain, absorb or delay crises. This includes the expansion of the spatial horizons of the capitalist system, for example, in the form of new (more profitable) spaces of production or new regional markets. Such a spatial expansion (or spatial fix) is perhaps one of the ways in which the capitalist system is able to postpone the collapse predicted by Marx. In this view, geographical space plays a crucial role in the workings of the capitalist system. Economic globalisation then can be seen as a process driven by the capitalist imperative to maintain and continuously expand the horizons of profitability.

Another Marxist concept that tries to capture the operation of the capitalist economy over space is that of *spatial divisions of labour*. It describes the way in which capitalism creates spatial structures that assign distinct economic functions to particular regions. The economic fortunes of these regions are thus linked to their position in the spatial division of labour within the wider economic structure. Related to this is a concept of 'core-periphery', which conceptualises uneven development as a set of uneven economic relations between a (dominant) core region and (dominated) periphery region(s). Somewhat echoing the exploitative nature of capitalist class relations, the 'core-periphery' concept suggests that rich regions (or countries) exist thanks to the exploitation of peripheral regions (or countries). One way or other, in Marxist-inspired approaches, uneven development is always linked to the structural features of the economy (see more in Chapter 5). Global inequalities thus can be seen as reflecting international division of labour between developed core and developing periphery (see more in Chapter 7). This kind of conceptualisation is in stark contrast to some alternative approaches that will be examined in turn.

Evolutionary-Institutionalist Approaches and 'new economic geography'

Economic geography approaches that draw from heterodox economics and the evolutionary-institutionalist perspective represent a diverse and evolving group (e.g., see Martin, 2002 for a good overview). However, some common features are discernible. As we have seen earlier in this chapter, the evolutionary-institutionalist perspective emphasises the importance of social, cultural and institutional factors for the understanding of the ways economies work. This is in contrast to both neo-classical views (that largely disregard such factors) and the Marxist approach (that assumes that such factors are determined by, rather than being determinants of, the economy). However, the evolutionary-institutionalist perspective sees the economy as always embedded in, and constituted by, social, cultural and institutional spheres. Economic geography approaches developed from this perspective thus see *uneven development as inextricably linked to (or shaped by) institutional contexts*. One of the key points that such economic geography approaches are making is that social, cultural and institutional contexts are *place-specific*. In other words, economic fortunes of regions (or whole countries) depend on the institutional arrangements that these regions (or countries) are able to create (see more in Chapter 6).

At the regional level, for instance, the concept of *institutional thickness* has been proposed to capture the strength of local/regional institutions, their ability to cooperate and to promote a coherent development strategy. In line with the view that successful economies are increasingly knowledge-based or learning economies, successful regions have also been conceptualised as *learning regions*. The key feature of such regions is their ability to innovate, to learn and to accumulate knowledge in various forms, thanks to their institutional set-up. It is argued, for instance, that the capacity to innovate and to learn depends on various collaborative networks, which are sustained thanks to the institutions of trust, shared culture and social capital, all of which are dependent on particular regional settings. In this view then, regions are in fact seen as key engines of the global knowledge economy and uneven development in such an economy is a result of differences in regional institutional thickness, innovation capacity, learning and knowledge accumulation.

Interestingly, there are two opposing views with regard to the prospect of achieving balanced development in the (global) knowledge-based or learning economy. The first view is based on the assumption that economically lagging regions (or nations) can catch up because favourable conditions for growth can be created locally by making appropriate institutional arrangements. This view is further supported by the assumption that knowledge (the key resource in the global knowledge economy) can now move freely around the world thanks to ICTs. It should therefore be possible for previously underdeveloped regions to emulate the success of leading regions such as Silicon Valley (see also Box 6.1 in Chapter 6). The implication of this line of argument is that the arrival of the global knowledge economy will help to overcome massive economic differences across the world.

The second, and opposing, view suggests that uneven development will continue to be a feature in the knowledge-based economy. This view is based on the assumption that the key sources of competitiveness and economic success is non-standardised *tacit* knowledge (as opposed to standardised, written, *explicit* knowledge). Tacit knowledge, the argument goes, is embedded in local/regional institutions, regional innovation cultures and *clusters* and these are apparently place-specific to the extent that they cannot be replicated by regions elsewhere. This would imply that globalisation will *not* automatically lead to the eradication of global inequalities.

One way or another, the interest in regional institutional settings has been associated with the emergence of so-called new economic geography – that is, an economic geography approach that moves away from viewing economic processes as separate from social, cultural and political contexts and emphasises that these contexts are crucial for understanding economic dynamics (e.g., see Coe et al., 2007, p.13; see Chapter 2 for a discussion of differences between new economic geography and New Economic Geography [NEG]). New economic geography therefore also enthusiastically embraces the notions of culture, social capital, ethnicity and gender in its study of the economy (e.g., see Lee and Wills, 1997), reflecting a wider 'cultural turn' in social sciences.

CONCLUSION

This chapter aimed to examine three interrelated questions, namely: (1) What is the economy?; (2) How does the economy work?; and (3) How does the economy work *over space*? In relation to the first question, the chapter argued that a definition of the economy is both problematic and contentious, not least because the question arises as to what is included in, and what is excluded from, being considered as an economic process. Further to this, the extent to which economic processes can be separated from cultural, social, political and environmental processes is another contentious issue.

In relation to the second and third questions, the chapter examined three contrasting perspectives on the economy (neo-classical, Marxist and alternative perspectives). The chapter emphasised that different perspectives on the economy have profound implications for the theoretical conceptualisation of economic geographies. Indeed, as highlighted by the chapter, there are stark differences between neo-classical, Marxist and alternative approaches to economic geographies. The neo-classical perspective supports the view that any uneven development is of a temporary nature and should melt away under the operation of market forces. The Marxist approach, in contrast, emphasises that uneven development is an inherent, structural and unavoidable feature of the capitalist economy. Alternative approaches, meanwhile, focus on institutional and cultural factors to account for uneven patterns of economic development.

All these approaches have their strengths and weaknesses, but they all offer some useful insights into the workings of economies in the global era. Therefore, they all deserve to be examined in more detail. Chapter 4 will take on the task of describing economic geography concepts developed from neo-classical foundations. Chapter 5 will further elaborate on the Marxist approach to the economy and will introduce key concepts that aim to explain uneven development. Chapter 6 will present alternative approaches and new economic geography.

FURTHER READING

Coe, N.M., P.F. Kelly and H.W.C. Yeung (2007) *Economic Geography: A Contemporary Introduction*. (Oxford: Blackwell) Chapters 2 and 3.

Hudson, R. (2005) *Economic Geographies: Circuits, Flows and Spaces*. (London: Sage) Chapter 1.

MacKinnon, D. and A. Cumbers (2007) *An Introduction to Economic Geography: Globalization, Uneven Development and Place*. (Harlow: Pearson/Prentice Hall) Chapters 2 and 3.

Martin, R. (2002) 'Institutional Approaches in Economic Geography', in E. Sheppard and T.J. Barnes (eds) *A Companion to Economic Geography*. (Malden, MA: Blackwell), pp.77–94.

Pike, A., A. Rodriguez-Pose and J. Tomaney (2006) *Local and Regional Development*. (London and New York: Routledge) Chapter 2.

USEFUL WEBSITES*

http://www.communityeconomies.org/Home – the Community Economies project website is a place where new visions of community and economy can be theorized, discussed, represented and enacted. The project grew out of J.K. Gibson-Graham's feminist critique of political economy that focused upon the limiting effects of representing economies as dominantly capitalist. Central to the project is the idea that economies are always diverse and always in the process of becoming. One of the aims of the Community Economies project is to produce a more inclusive understanding of economy.

http://www.econlib.org/index.html – the Library of Economics and Liberty is dedicated to advancing the study of economics, markets and liberty. It offers a unique combination of resources for students, teachers, researchers and aficionados of economic thought. The website is provided by Liberty Fund, Inc., a private, educational foundation established to encourage the study of the ideal of a society of free and responsible individuals. The site includes access to the online *Concise Encyclopedia of Economics* (CEE): http://www.econlib. org/library/CEE.html. As an observant reader you will notice that much of the material on this website is US-centred and frequently written from a particular (free-market) perspective.

http://www.newschool.edu/nssr/economics/ – the History of Economic Thought (HET) website provided by the Economics Department at the New School for Social Research (New York) includes useful materials on key economic thinkers, theories and schools of thought.

* All accessed 1 March 2011.

4.   Neo-classical approach, location theory and beyond

INTRODUCTION

As seen in the previous chapter, one can identify three main theoretical approaches on the economy – neo-classical, Marxist and alternative approaches. Each of these approaches has different answers to questions of how economies work and how economies work over space. Each of these approaches is thus associated with a different set of economic geography theories and concepts. This chapter will examine theories and concepts in economic geography that use the mainstream (neo-classical) perspective of the economy as their starting point. It will start by examining the hypothesis of the spatial equilibrium and will proceed to examine concepts and theories that demonstrate that uneven development is a more likely outcome of the operation of market forces.

The chapter will be organised in the following way. The first section will include a discussion on the neo-classical spatial equilibrium hypothesis, which presupposes that factors of production (capital and labour) will disperse across regions to create a balanced and efficient pattern of development. This would support the view that any uneven development is temporary and will disappear in the future thanks to the operation of market forces. The subsequent section will offer a discussion on neo-classical location theories, with a particular focus on central place theory, the concept of market potential and that of connectivity-accessibility. The central place theory shows that even under perfect market conditions economic activities will cluster in certain locations (central places), creating a dynamic equilibrium in space and a distinct urban hierarchy. Such an urban hierarchy, in turn, creates different levels of market potential and connectivity-accessibility, with important implications for the location of economic activities. Finally, the chapter will turn attention to the concepts of agglomeration economies and increasing returns and the theory of cumulative causation, all of which help to explain why the spatial equilibrium envisaged by the neo-classical theory is hard to achieve. These latter concepts demonstrate that rather than having a self-correcting dispersal effect, market forces can in fact reinforce existing inequalities in space. The conclud-ing section will discuss the implications of these findings for uneven development in the global age.

NEO-CLASSICAL SPATIAL EQUILIBRIUM

The simplest version of the neo-classical spatial model involves the movement across space of the two key factors of production – capital and labour. Imagine a country – an island – that has two regions, one 'rich' and one 'poor' (Figure 4.1a). In the rich region, there is a great supply of capital, but a relative shortage of labour. As a result of this labour shortage, the wages in the rich region will be very high. In the poor region, wages are much lower, due to the abundance of labour and a relative lack of capital. According to the neo-classical model, labour will move from the poor region to the rich region in search of higher wages, while the capital will move in the opposite direction in search of cheaper labour (and thus higher profits; see Figure 4.1b). This is fully in line with the expected behaviour of a rational 'economic man'. Importantly, individual actions of this kind will ensure that the system as a whole will reach *spatial equilibrium* (Figure 4.1c). The economic geographer, Diane Perrons, summarises the neo-classical hypothesis as follows:

> Labour and capital are predicted to move from areas of surplus to areas of deficit, stimulated by higher returns – wages or profits respectively. Thus, labour should move from poor to rich regions and capital should move in the opposite direction until wages and profits are equalised across regions resulting in an efficient and balanced pattern of development. (Perrons, 2004, p.56)

Even more complex neo-classical models that involve other factors of production (e.g., technology) are all built around the assumption that some sort of spatial equilibrium will be achieved in the long run, because such factors of production will inevitably spread or disperse over space. To some extent, the processes of spatial dispersal can indeed be observed in reality, both within countries (see below) and at global scale (e.g., see Chapter 7). However, the examples of spatial equilibrium that the neo-classical theory envisages are hard to find. Firms, for instance, do not just disperse over space but cluster in particular locations. The explanation for this has been offered by the neo-classical location theory, which will be examined in turn.

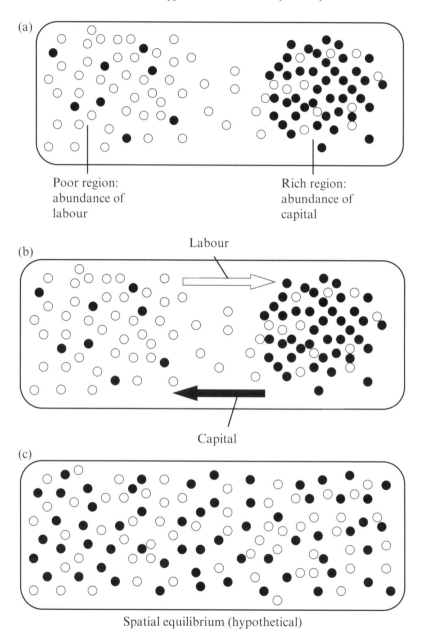

Source: Illustration by Martin Sokol.

Figure 4.1   Neo-classical spatial equilibrium

NEO-CLASSICAL LOCATION THEORY

One way of accounting for the fact that spatial equilibrium does not occur, is to acknowledge that in real life, factors of production cannot move 'freely' over space. Indeed, there are various constraints involved. One of the obvious obstacles is the *friction of distance*. In other words, moving people, machinery, materials or goods over geographical distance usually involves a cost. For workers, there is usually a price tag associated with travelling to work, for instance. For firms, there is a cost involved in moving raw materials from the source to the factory and there is a cost associated with delivering finished products from the factory to consumers (i.e., literally bringing them to market). Thus, for both people and businesses, location in space is a crucial part of their strategy of self-interest and profit-maximisation. The calculation of the cost associated with moving across space and the implication of this for location in space, forms the basis of the neo-classical location theory. Key concepts that build upon the location theory include central place theory, urban hierarchy, market potential and connectivity-accessibility, all of which will be explored in turn.

Central Place Theory and Urban Hierarchy

Central place theory helps us to understand how the friction of distance influences the pattern of the location of economic activities in space, while focusing on the issue of the delivery of goods and services from producers/providers to customers/clients. In order to explain central place theory, let's return to our imaginary island. The starting point of central place theory is the observation that even if the population (consumers) of the island were distributed evenly over space, firms (producers) would still tend to cluster in particular locations (Figure 4.2a). Walter Christaller, a German scholar and the key proponent of central place theory called these locations *central places*. Why would firms want to locate in central places? The friction of distance, and the cost associated with overcoming it, is the central element in the explanation offered by location theorists (e.g., von Thünen [1826] 1966; Weber, 1929; Christaller [1933] 1966; Lösh [1935] 1954; Isard, 1956). Central place theory highlights the fact that firms do not simply have 'markets' – they have 'market areas'. Geography is a factor in the operation of the market, because there are transport costs associated with delivering finished products (i.e., pins, shoes or sausages) to customers. The longer the delivery distance, the higher the final price of a product (final price = production cost + transport cost). In order for a firm to survive, it clearly needs a certain minimum market area. The

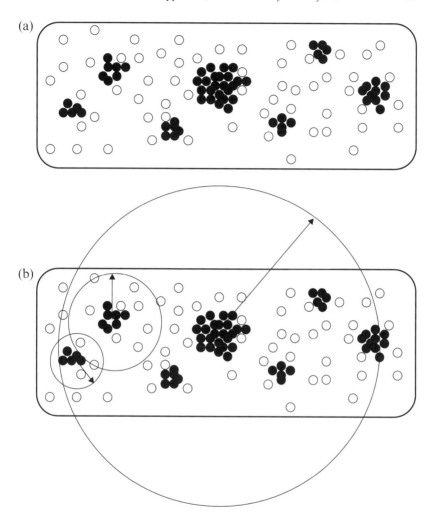

Source: Illustration by Martin Sokol.

Figure 4.2   Central place theory: hierarchy of central places

pin-making factory, for instance, needs a certain minimum market area to be viable. This minimum market area must contain a sufficient number of potential customers that would create a sufficient demand for its products (pins). This minimum market area is called *threshold*. Of course, it is in the interest of every factory to extend its market area well beyond the threshold. However, due to the transport costs, a market area cannot be infinitely large. Indeed, with each mile or kilometre of distance from the factory, the final price of a product (e.g., a box of pins) will increase. Following the neo-classical reasoning of supply and demand, with each price increase, the number of customers willing to pay for the product will decrease. As the price of our box of pins increases with distance, fewer and fewer customers will be willing to pay for it, until we reach a point where a box of pins becomes too expensive for anyone to buy it. In central place theory this is called a *market area range*. Beyond the range, there is no market for our pins due to the transport costs involved. It goes without saying that for a company to be profitable, the market area range must be bigger than the threshold. In general, the bigger the overall market area, the better.

However, central place theory rightly points out that different products (and services) have market areas of different sizes. In fact, one can imagine a hierarchy of goods and services, each having different market areas and therefore prompting a different location in space for their providers. A simple ranking may include higher-order, medium-order and lower-order goods and services. Higher-order goods would include high-value items that are bought infrequently (e.g., cars). Lower-order goods would include the least expensive items that customers demand on a frequent basis (e.g., milk). According to this logic, butchers, bakers, pin-makers, shoe-makers, car-makers would locate in central places of relevant order, because those locations offer the best opportunity to serve the market (Figure 4.2b).

What central place theory does then, is apply the principles of neo-classical thought to location in space, while incorporating the role of geographical distance (in the form of transport costs). In doing so, it shows that spatial equilibrium characterised by the total dispersal of economic activities is unlikely to happen. However, the theory remains firmly within the neo-classical framework. It suggests that an equilibrium will emerge out of the balance between the input of money (i.e., demand from the population) and the outputs of goods and services (i.e., supply by producers). In this particular instance, locational theorists talk about a *dynamic* equilibrium. A dynamic equilibrium will be achieved as firms move around and locate in central places until the island is covered by overlapping market areas of various hierarchical order, ensuring that demand by local consumers is met by producers' supply in the most efficient manner (see Dicken and Lloyd, 1990, p.38; Coe et al., 2007, pp.291–2, Box 10.2 and Figure 10.1).

One important implication of the central place theory model is that the hierarchy of central places can be translated into an *urban hierarchy*. Higher-order central places become higher-order urban centres, while lower-order central places correspond to lower-order settlements. A simple urban hierarchy that can emerge out of Christaller's conceptualisation of central places may involve five levels, namely:

1.   metropolis;
2.   city;
3.   town;
4.   village;
5.   hamlet (see Dicken and Lloyd, 1990, p.28).

While central place theory does represent a major improvement on the original simple spatial equilibrium model, it has its own shortcomings. One of the key limits (already recognised by central place theorists such as August Lösh [1935] 1954 and Walter Isard, 1956) is that population is never spread evenly over space. Rather, population is likely to concentrate in urban centres of various sizes, perhaps reflecting the urban hierarchy outlined above. This also means that market opportunities are not spread evenly over space. This in turn, may have important implications for the location of firms. One concept that is used to capture this is called market potential and this will be examined in turn alongside the concepts of connectivity and accessibility.

Market Potential and Connectivity-Accessibility

Connectivity-accessibility, in its simplest terms, can be defined as the ease with which people, materials and information can be moved from one location to another (e.g., within and between regions). In contemporary economies, these movements are usually supported by dedicated transport infrastructure (e.g., rail, road, air, water) and telecommunication networks (e.g., telephone, telegraph, Internet). Therefore, regional connectivity-accessibility could also be seen as a measure of the ability of these infrastructures and networks to reduce the friction of distance within and between regions. While the two terms (connectivity and accessibility) are often used interchangeably, there are in fact subtle differences between the concept of connectivity and the concept of accessibility (Sokol, 2009).

Connectivity (sometimes also referred to as *connectedness*) usually relates to the features of a given transport or communications network and can be measured in two basic ways. The first one is to measure the level of connectivity of an entire network (i.e., the degree to which the network as a whole is internally connected). Numerous indices have been devised to measure such connectivity. One of the most frequently used is the *beta index*, which is calculated as the ratio of links (connections) to nodes (e.g., urban centres). The higher the number of links to nodes, the

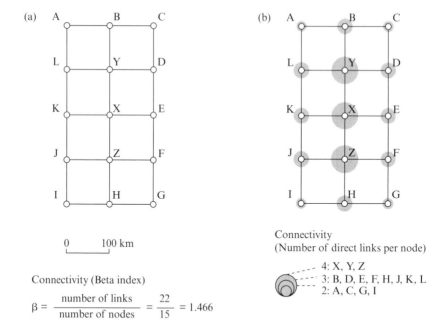

Connectivity (Beta index)

$$\beta = \frac{\text{number of links}}{\text{number of nodes}} = \frac{22}{15} = 1.466$$

Source: Adapted from Sokol (2009).

Figure 4.3   Connectivity

higher the degree of connectivity of a given network. Figure 4.3a shows an example of a calculation of beta index for our imaginary island, which has 15 urban centres (nodes) connected by a simple road network grid (links).

The second option is to measure the level of connectivity of individual places (nodes) within a network. In other words, node connectivity measures the degree to which individual nodes are connected with other nodes within the network. Again, this can be done in a number of ways. The simplest measure of node connectivity is the number of direct links that a particular node has with other nodes. The more direct links a particular node has, the higher its degree of connectivity (see Figure 4.3b). The measures of connectivity may be useful in some cases and some firms may choose to locate in certain places thanks to their higher level of connectivity (e.g., for a multi-national corporation, a number of direct flights to the largest pool of destinations may be important). However, if firms want to achieve the best possible access to the largest share of markets, then the concepts of accessibility and market potential may be more relevant for their location decisions.

The concept of *accessibility* is based on the explicit recognition of the importance of both the geographical distances between nodes (e.g., urban centres) *and* the characteristics of the nodes. The characteristics of the nodes are sometimes called the 'attributes of destinations' (see below). Within the concept of accessibility, the aspect of geographical distance (i.e., the length of links between the nodes) is considered as an *impedance* to the movement of people, materials and information. While transport and tel-ecommunication infrastructures may reduce the friction of distance, it still takes a certain amount of time, money and/or effort to move people, goods and services around. Travel time and travel cost are often a direct function of the distance covered (although, this does not always hold true). One way or another, the level of impedance is clearly important to economic agents, as we have already learned in the case of central place theory.

The crucial difference is that the concept of accessibility explicitly recog-nises the fact that population (and therefore market) is not evenly spread over space. The attributes of destinations (i.e., the level of attractiveness of nodes) represent the second dimension of the concept of accessibility. From an economic point of view, the level of attractiveness of destina-tions is frequently associated with the size of their markets, which can be expressed as an *economic mass* or volume of economic activity either in terms of population size, income, spending power, gross domestic product (GDP), opportunities to be reached, or similar characteristics. This is based on an assumption that the bigger the market a firm has access to, the better the prospects for the firm's profitability and growth. This way, the level of accessibility (to markets) is directly associated with the expected economic performance and competitiveness of firms. In other words, it is expected that a firm (e.g., the pin-making business) will be more suc-cessful if it locates in places (regions) with high levels of accessibility. In turn, regions with high levels of accessibility are expected to be more economically viable.

This assumption is encapsulated in the *market potential* or *economic potential* model, which represents the most frequent way of measuring accessibility (see Sokol, 2009). In this model, the economic potential of a region is a positive function of the size of markets (economic mass) that can be accessed from the region, and a negative function of impedance (e.g., geographical distance) that needs to be overcome when reaching those markets. In the simplest measure of regional accessibility, the poten-tial of any region can be calculated by summing the population of all other regions in the system and dividing these by some measure of their interven-ing distance. The potential of region *i*, thus can be calculated as:

$$Pi = (j = 1 \rightarrow j = n) \, \Sigma Mj \, / \, Dij$$

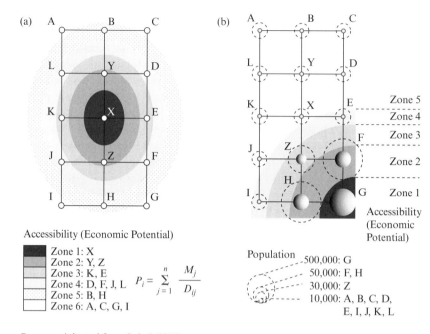

Source: Adapted from Sokol (2009).

Figure 4.4   Market potential and accessibility

where Pi is the potential of region i, Mj is a measure of economic mass (e.g., population) in region j and Dij is a measure of impedance (distance) from region i to region j and n is the total number of regions in the system. The regions located closest to the biggest markets (and therefore presumably having the cheapest access to them) would be seen as having the highest economic potential. The way in which the size of markets (economic mass) influences the market potential of different places is captured in Figure 4.4. If all the urban centres on our island were of equal size (e.g., towns with populations of 10,000 each) then the picture of accessibility measured through the market potential model (with population as a measure of economic mass) would be simple: the urban centres located in the geographical centre of the island would display the highest level of accessibility. Meanwhile the urban centres located at the geographical periphery of the island would be considered as the least accessible (see Figure 4.4a).

However, if, for whatever reason, the populations of these urban centres start to vary, the picture of accessibility can change considerably, due to the changing market potential. If, for instance, urban centre G were to become a city with a population of 500,000, the picture of accessibility for this regional economy would be dramatically transformed. Indeed, city G with its population of half a million people would several times exceed the population (market size) of the rest of the island. Therefore, due to the weight of its own self-potential (however calculated), city G (formerly one of the least accessible places) would become the most accessible place on the island (all this without changing the levels of connectivity). Thanks to their proximity to city G, urban centres F and H, would overnight become the second-best 'accessible' places on the island, perhaps attracting some population growth, thus further strengthening their own market potential, while having a similar knock-on effect on town Z (see Figure 4.4b). Looking at the question of industrial location from the point of view of market potential and regional accessibility, our pin-making factory will be best located in city G, where the biggest market can be reached with the least effort or cost.

As we can see from the above example, the economic mass (i.e., the size of market) has a major influence on the level of accessibility of different regions. The concept of market potential using two variables (impedance and economic mass) is ultimately more satisfactory than Christaller's concept of central places, which operates with one variable (impedance) only. The concept of market potential, in other words, helps us to better understand the economic pull that is created when markets are being concentrated in particular places. Further insights into why economic activities simply do not disperse in space are offered by the concepts of agglomeration economies and cumulative causation, which will be examined in turn.

AGGLOMERATION ECONOMIES AND CUMULATIVE CAUSATION

Agglomeration Economies

As noted above, the market potential model is based on the assumption that the bigger the market a firm has access to, the better the prospects for the firm's profitability and growth. But this is not the end of the story. By pursuing the strategy of locating close to (or directly within) large markets, firms inevitably end up locating close to each other. This, in itself, can be a source of additional advantage. Indeed, *firms can derive further advantages (additional benefits) from simply co-locating in particular places.* In other words 'clustering itself offers further economies' (Dicken and Lloyd, 1990, p.207). Economies ('savings') derived from co-located firms are called *agglomeration economies* or *economies of agglomeration*. In order to explain how agglomeration economies work, we will introduce the concepts of economies of scale and increasing returns to scale.

Let us start with the concept of *economies of scale* (or *scale economies*). There are two types of scale economies – *internal* economies of scale (i.e., scale economies internal to the firm) and *external* economies of scale (i.e., scale economies derived from factors outside the firm). In order to explain how internal economies of scale work, let us return to our pin-making factory. As we have already learned in Chapter 3, Adam Smith described a situation in which major productivity gains were achieved by introducing a division of labour (i.e., by assigning workers to particular specialised tasks). There are about 18 specialised tasks to be performed in the pin-making process. One worker alone would find it difficult to produce one pin a day (and certainly not 20). However, productivity can increase dramatically if ten workers are employed to do the job. It could be argued that further productivity gains are possible if 18 workers were employed, each performing just one particular task. Internal economies have emerged in our pin-making factory thanks to the division of labour. Importantly, these economies ('savings') have been growing as we have been up-scaling our production, by employing more and more workers. The bigger the operation (the more workers we have employed), the higher productivity per worker has been achieved (thus giving us higher *rates of profit* or *return* to our investment). In other words, we have achieved *increasing returns to scale*.

Unfortunately, returns to scale are not increasing indefinitely. One can imagine that our pin-making factory can employ more workers still. For instance, a cleaner, a machine repair specialist, an accountant, advertising/marketing people and selling agent(s) may all come in useful. Also, employing a worker responsible for delivering boxes of pins to our customers in our market area would be of benefit. So, one can imagine that the factory can probably profitably employ up to 23 or 25 workers, although the *profit per worker* can start to decline (i.e., we would start experiencing *decreasing returns to scale*). Beyond a certain employee level, the return to scale would start to decline dramatically. In other words, we would not gain much by employing additional workers as the existing workforce is already covering all the tasks in an efficient manner. In fact, employing an extra pair of hands would probably be more of a hindrance than a benefit – the profit per worker would plummet. In other words, we would experience dramatically decreasing or *diminishing returns to scale*. Given that the profit is the most important imperative for firms in the market economy, the ratio between the level of investment and level of profit derived from such an investment (i.e., the *rate of profit*) needs to be watched closely.

Consider now what options are available to firms if they 'cluster' (co-locate) in certain locations. It is possible that if such a geographical concentration (or agglomeration) of firms was large enough, certain specialised tasks can be performed by specialist firms. For instance, there may be scope for a professional accountant who can provide comprehensive accountancy services to all firms in the agglomeration – and at a much smaller cost to the firms involved. Our pin-making factory would benefit from this, because the need to employ our own full-time accountant would disappear (thus saving us money and increasing our profit). Similar economies can be achieved if other tasks or sub-processes were performed by specialist firms, rather than employing in-house workers. One can imagine that a cleaning company, a machine repair company, an advertising agency or a transport (courier) company can be set up if sufficient demand exists within the agglomeration. In effect, division of labour (between firms) would emerge in such an agglomeration. The benefits of such a division of labour between firms would be similar to those derived from a division of labour within firms. Economies of scale can be realised, but this time these economies would be *external* to any one firm. Our pin-making factory would benefit from this development and its profitability would increase. In other words, our pin-making factory (as well as other producers in the agglomeration) would reap the benefits of *agglomeration economies*.

Such benefits of agglomeration were originally described more than a century ago by Alfred Marshall in *Principles of Economics* [1890] (2009). Marshall also argued that, in addition to agglomerated firms providing each other with key inputs and markets (as described above), there are two further major benefits of agglomeration (or of an 'industrial district'). First, the availability of a local pool of skilled labour may be an advantage, and second, firms within an agglomeration may benefit from knowledge spillovers (i.e., knowledge exchanged between firms). This latter point about knowledge spillovers is interesting, because it diverts from a strict neo-classical framework. More recently, it has been re-discovered by the new economic geography approaches that we will discuss later in the book.

Meanwhile, you will find that literature usually describes two types of agglomeration economies – *localisation economies* and *urbanisation economies* (e.g., see Dicken and Lloyd, 1990, pp.211–12; Coe et al., 2007, p.137). Localisation economies are agglomeration economies that emerge between specialised suppliers, collaborators, sub-contractors or competitors within a single industry (e.g., pin-making industry, steel industry or financial services industry) located together in a particular place. Urbanisation economies, on the other hand, refer to agglomeration economies shared by all firms in all industries in one location (e.g., urban agglomeration). In real life, localisation economies and urbanisation economies are sometimes hard to distinguish, as the boundaries between these two notions are rather porous. One way or another, firms co-locating in particular locations can often benefit from agglomeration economies, which can include (see Dicken and Lloyd, 1990, pp.207–18; Smith, 1994a, p.4; 1994b, pp.184–5):

- the collective use of transport infrastructure and communication facilities;
- the local availability of skilled labour force;
- a technical college or university offering relevant training;
- access to research facilities;
- proximity to ancillary industries (materials, components, machinery, specialised services – such as those described above), among others.

Further to this, it is important to recognise that agglomerations are usually underpinned by two types of linkages (or *interdependencies*) between firms. The first type is referred to as traded interdependencies, the second one as untraded interdependencies (see Coe et al., 2007, pp.137–43). *Traded interdependencies* are created by firms having formal trading relationships between them within a given agglomeration. For instance, our pin-making factory has a formal contractual relationship with a professional accountant, with a cleaning company, or with a local courier service. These arrangements benefit from agglomeration economies as described above. On the other hand, *untraded interdependencies* refer to the less tangible benefits of being located in the same place. Untraded interdependencies may include various informal links and interactions between firms and between firms and other economic actors. Untraded interdependencies thus relate to various social and cultural bases of agglomerations that go beyond the narrow neo-classical definitions of the 'economic'. The concept of untraded interdependencies is linked to the notion of clusters, which will be examined in more detail in Chapter 6, alongside the alternative and new economic geography approaches.

Cumulative Causation

As seen from the discussion above, important advantages (economies) occur for firms locating close to each other in specific locations. We can now ask the question: what are the implications of this for uneven development? The theory of cumulative causation introduced by a Swedish scholar Gunnar Myrdal (1957; see also Kaldor 1970, 1989) argues that a circular chain reaction will emerge, leading to a greater polarisation between rich (core) and poor (economically peripheral) regions. In the rich regions with strong agglomeration economies, a virtuous circle of growth and development may emerge in which 'success breeds success'. In part, this is possible thanks to the *multiplier effect* (see Dicken and Lloyd, 1990, pp.222–34), a mechanism in which each dollar spent in the local economy generates further income down the line. Indeed, it is not difficult to imagine that existing agglomeration economies may attract further firms into the region (or allow for the expansion of existing firms). If this happens then a circular chain reaction will begin. Indeed, jobs created by new or expanding firms will increase employment and the population of the region. This in turn will increase local demand for goods and services, thus leading to an enlarged local supply base and expanded service sector. This in turn will enlarge the local financial (tax) base and spending power of the local government, which will allow for local infrastructure to be upgraded. This in turn will increase agglomeration economies. The increased agglomeration economies will again attract more firms into the region, fuelling a virtuous circle of growth and development (see Dicken and Lloyd, 1990, pp.219–52; Pike et al., 2006, pp.73–4). This is then a principle of *circular and cumulative causation* in which one event triggers a sequence of causal links in a circular and self-reinforcing way.

What we observe could also be described as a process of increasing returns to scale, although this time at the level of the entire agglomeration. If in operation, such a process would ensure that the bigger the agglomeration gets, the bigger the agglomeration economies that can be achieved. In addition to the advantages described above, such a growing agglomeration may go hand in hand with an increasingly diverse economic base characterised by a complex division of labour. Indeed, as a given agglomeration grows, there is a possibility that more and more specialised tasks will be carried out by specialist firms, contributing to the increasing division of labour between firms, thus increasing economies of agglomeration further still.

While the increasing dynamism of successful regions may be welcome, the problem is that their expansion may be happening at the expense of other regions. Indeed, it may well be the case that firms that are being attracted by the vibrant economic climate of large agglomerations relocate there from poorer, 'less developed' or less favoured regions. The loss of a firm in a less favoured region generates a negative chain reaction that mirrors the process of cumulative causation in an adverse sense. Indeed, it is not difficult to imagine that the closure of a firm leads to the loss of employment and possibly to a loss of population too, via out-migration. Either way, the spending power of the local population decreases, reducing

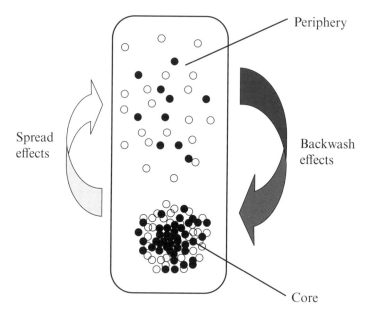

Periphery

Spread
effects

Backwash
effects

Core

Source: Illustration by Martin Sokol.

Figure 4.5   Cumulative causation

the local demand for goods and services and in turn undermining the local
tax base, leading to the reduced ability of the local government to maintain
local infrastructure. This, in turn, affects the agglomeration economies
and reduces the attractiveness of the peripheral region further still. More
firms may choose to relocate to richer (core) regions, and the younger and
skilled workforce may follow suit. In essence, this constitutes what Myrdal
called a *backwash effect* – a flow of capital and labour from lagging regions
to developed regions. Contrary to the neo-classical assumption of spatial
equilibrium, the backwash effect will cause the economic gap between
rich and poor regions to widen further (Figure 4.5). The rich (advanced)
regions will end up with increasing levels of investment, young workers,
growing purchasing power and improving local services and infrastructure, while less developed regions will be characterised by a lack of investment, an ageing labour force, a decline in local services and a dilapidated
infrastructure. This polarised spatial pattern is often referred to as *core-
periphery* (e.g., see Krugman, 1991). The important question is whether
such a core-periphery pattern will remain in place once established.

   This is a difficult question. Some economists and economic geographers believe that just as is the case with individual firms, agglomerations too have their limits, beyond which diminishing returns will kick in. Indeed, the *dis-economies* that may occur in large cities may include the prohibitive cost of land, the cost of labour, pollution and congestion. Such dis-economies may indeed encourage the decentralisation of operations or whole firms to less developed regions. In other words, *spread effects* may emerge, as predicted by the neo-classical spatial equilibrium model. However, according to cumulative causation theorists, backwash effects (centripetal forces) will always be greater than spread effects (centrifugal forces), thus contributing to the polarisation, rather than the dispersal, of economic fortunes between regions. This is because: 'market forces, if left to their own devices, are spatially disequilibriating. Economies of scale and agglomeration lead to the cumulative concentration of capital, labour, and output in certain regions at the expense of others: uneven regional development is self-reinforcing' (Martin and Sunley, 1998, p.201; cited in Pike at al., 2006, p.70).

In essence, the theory of cumulative causation provides further evidence that, rather than having a self-correcting effect, *market forces can in fact reinforce existing inequalities in space*. The kind of spatial equilibrium envisaged by neo-classical theory (introduced at the beginning of this chapter) is therefore difficult to achieve. Importantly, this conclusion has been reached while using the neo-classical conceptual framework (e.g., profit-maximising agents, market operation, price signals, etc.). It could therefore be argued that the cumulative causation theory and similar concepts 'use the approach and language of neo-classical economics to reach contrary conclusions' (Pike et al., 2006, p.70).

CONCLUSION

This chapter has aimed to provide an introduction to key concepts and theories in economic geography whose starting point is the mainstream economic (neo-classical) perspective. The chapter started by examining the hypothesis of spatial equilibrium and proceeded to examine concepts that demonstrate that spatially uneven development is a more likely outcome of the operation of market forces. These findings have important implications for the debate about spatial inequalities in the global era. Indeed, many arguments about the positive effects that economic globalisation can achieve in less developed countries are based on the assumption of the hypothetical spatial equilibrium that is supposed to emerge if market forces are allowed to operate around the globe.

A similar set of arguments is underpinning the economic rationale of the

European Union (EU) too. Indeed, the removal of internal borders and other barriers within the EU aims to create one big marketplace with a free movement of people (labour), money (capital), goods and services across Europe (see also Chapter 7). Many believe that such a common European market will ultimately benefit everybody involved. This is based on the assumption that the free movement of people, capital, goods and services will lead to a more efficient organisation of the European economy *and* that more balanced patterns of economic development will emerge across Europe. In other words, many believe that economic efficiency achieved at the European level will be accompanied by increased territorial equality between Europe's regions – a point hotly debated.

Regardless, many global enthusiasts believe that such positive results can be achieved at the global level also. In fact, some would argue that positive effects of the 'invisible hand' of the market can be felt even with an incomplete set of factors of production moving around. The argument goes that economic globalisation will benefit everybody by simply allowing a free movement of goods and services (free trade) and a free movement of capital only – that is, without even having a free movement of labour! Indeed, much of the globalising efforts of international organisations in the last several decades have concentrated on making the movements of capital and trade freer across the globe (see also Chapter 7). This, combined with the continually improving transport capability (dramatically increasing speed and decreasing cost of moving things around the world), would imply that economic activities can be more evenly spread over the world (as capital would seek cheaper locations to produce). Some would argue that the decreasing cost of transport also means that the agglomeration forces described in this chapter may be weakening. At the extreme this would mean that agglomerations (cities) are no longer needed and that pre-existing concentrations of economic activity would disperse, creating a more balanced development pattern. However, the available evidence suggests that cities continue to be major nodes of economic activity and that global inequalities are growing. This could either mean that the processes of agglomeration and cumulative causation described in this chapter are still in operation (perhaps at a global level), or that another/alternative set of forces is shaping economic geographies of globalisation. The following chapter will explore one such alternative view.

FURTHER READING

Dicken, P. and P. Lloyd (1990) *Location in Space: Theoretical Perspectives in Economic Geography.* (New York: Harper Collins Publishers) Chapters 1 and 2 on central place theory and urban hierarchy; Chapter 3 on transportation costs; Chapter 5 on market potential and agglomeration economies; Chapter 6 on cumulative causation.

Pike, A., A. Rodriguez-Pose and J. Tomaney (2006) *Local and Regional Development*. (London and New York: Routledge) Chapter 3: sections on neo-classical theory, increasing returns and cumulative causation.

Sokol M. (2009), 'Regional Connectivity', in R. Kitchin and N. Thrift (eds) *International Encyclopedia of Human Geography*, Volume 9. (Oxford: Elsevier) pp.165–80, on market potential and connectivity-accessibility.

5. Marxist-inspired approaches and uneven development

INTRODUCTION

In the previous chapter we have examined concepts and theories of spatial development whose starting point is the neo-classical framework of self-interest and the profit-maximising behaviour of economic agents (e.g., firms). We have seen that after a thorough application of neo-classical principles, the original neo-classical ideal of spatial equilibrium is in fact hard to achieve. Some of these concepts and theories (e.g., the theory of cumulative causation) show that market forces can reinforce, rather than reduce, existing inequalities in space.

The issue of unequal and uneven development will be taken further in this chapter, although from a completely different perspective. The section will examine concepts and theories associated with the (broadly defined) Marxist perspective. This will include a discussion on wealth, value and circuits of capital, with an emphasis on the concepts and theories that help to elucidate the circuits of capital over space. Subsequently, the related concept of spatial (spatio-temporal) fix will be examined, highlighting the role of space and uneven development as fundamental to the functioning of the capitalist economy. Further to this the concept of spatial divisions of labour will be introduced alongside a discussion on the technical and social division of labour. The concept of the spatial divisions of labour helps us to appreciate how the economic fortunes of regions are associated with their position in the spatial division of labour within the wider economic structure. The chapter will conclude by examining the core-periphery concept, which conceptualises uneven development as a set of uneven economic relations between a (dominant) core region and (dominated) periphery regions.

WEALTH, VALUE AND CIRCUITS OF CAPITAL

In order to understand the Marxist conceptualisation of uneven development, it is important to examine the notions of wealth, value and circuits of capital in bit more detail. Let's start with *wealth*. Wealth can be defined as 'a cumulative share of the rewards created in the economic process of adding *value*' (Coe et al., 2007, p.64; original emphasis). The creation of value is therefore central to the discussion on economic development in general and uneven development in particular. But what is value and how is value created? As we have already learned in Chapter 3, according to Marxist theory, all value ultimately comes from human labour. In other words, 'value is always created by *people*' (ibid.; original emphasis) such as our workers in the pin-making factory. Workers engage in a labour process, that is, they apply their labour on raw materials (or semi-finished goods) to produce new goods (e.g., pins, shoes, clothes, cars, etc.) and these goods embody values.

Marxist theory distinguishes several types of value embodied in commodities. The key distinction can be made between exchange value and use value (see, for example, Craib, 1997, p.93). As we have already hinted in Chapter 3, *exchange value* is a value expressed in money for which a particular commodity has been sold on the market. A pair of shoes, a coat, a bottle of milk or an apple can all be commodities for which you need to pay a certain price (exchange value) to buy them. *Use value*, on the other hand, is the value of a commodity to the person who uses it – the pleasure, for instance, of drinking a glass of milk. Use value is therefore harder to express in terms of money. For instance, a coat can be bought via the Internet for the same price anywhere around the world (plus the delivery cost of course!), but the use value of having such a coat and keeping oneself warm is definitely higher for those living in cold climates.

For Marxists, the key problem of the capitalist system is that labour power itself is a commodity that is bought and sold on the market for an exchange value (i.e., wages). A capitalist (e.g., the pin-making factory owner) only employs workers if their use value to him or her (the value of what these workers produce for him or her) is greater than the exchange value of their labour (the wages that the capitalist has to pay to the workers; ibid., p.94). The difference between the two is surplus value. Capitalists accumulate wealth by appropriating surplus value through the exploitation of workers. Capitalists have to do this if they are to survive competition from their rivals. The creation of the little '*s*' (surplus value) is absolutely essential for the operation of the capitalist system and this is done via a *circuit of capital*, which we have described earlier (see Figure 3.3 in Chapter 3).

However, capitalists need to make a decision about what to do with the little '*s*' they 'create' (or, to be more precise, appropriate). One option is to simply consume it, for example, by indulging in the luxuries of life. This creates a situation that Marxists call a *simple reproduction* (Figure 5.1;

Source: Illustration by Martin Sokol.

Figure 5.1   *Circuit of capital: simple reproduction*

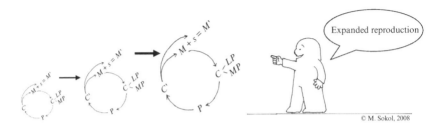

Source: Illustration by Martin Sokol.

Figure 5.2   *Circuit of capital: expanded reproduction*

see also Hudson, 2005, p.27). The other option is to re-invest the surplus value in the production process. For instance, the owner of the pin-making factory may decide to use the profit to hire a few more workers (the gains that can be achieved from the up-scaling of production in this way have been discussed in the previous chapter). In other words, the owner will engage in *expanded reproduction* (Hudson, 2005, p.27). With each run of the circuit of capital, the little '*s*' gets bigger and bigger (Figure 5.2). The rate at which surplus value is expanding is usually referred to as *accumulation* (of capital).

What we have just described is a circulation of value in the *primary circuit of capital*. The re-investment of surplus value in production involves continuously putting capital to work within the primary circuit of capital. This can work well, but there are limits. Indeed, as we have already learned, the capitalist system is crisis-prone. It is likely that, sooner or later, a crisis of *overaccumulation* will surface. This can happen in a number of ways, but usually such a crisis is caused by *over-production* (high levels of stock) and/or *under-consumption* (declining demand). In other words, too many pins or cars will be produced and too few people will be able to afford them. One way or another, the crisis of overaccumulation will mean falling rates of profit for the capitalist. The circuit of capital is broken, the surplus value cannot be created. Existing surplus value has nowhere to go to be profitably employed. The way in which the capitalist system copes with this has been described by economic geographer David Harvey in his influential book *The Limits to Capital* (Harvey, 1982), a new edition of which was published more recently (Harvey, 2006). Let us examine David Harvey's hypothesis in a bit more detail.

As already discussed in Chapter 3, one obvious 'solution' to the crisis of overaccumulation is *devaluation* (see also more below). However, Harvey has pointed out that another way of coping with this is *capital switching*. Capital switching involves re-directing capital surpluses to various other circuits of capital. This can happen at various levels and scales. It may be possible that profitable opportunities still exist within the primary circuit of capital. If a pin-making business goes bust, capital can be redirected to a mobile phone business; if a car-making business is in difficulty, money can be invested in the production of computers. Capitalists do not care which business their money is in, unless it produces the precious little '*s*'. However, if the crisis engulfs the entire economy, then switching capital within the primary circuit is not going to help (all producers are in trouble). The system then enters a 'switching crisis'.

However, David Harvey (1982, 2006) has identified two other circuits in which capital can be invested (see also Harvey, 1978): secondary and tertiary circuits of capital. The *secondary circuit* involves investing surplus value in *fixed capital*. Fixed capital includes all the elements of the built environment such as factories, dams, offices, shops, warehouses, roads, railways, docks, power stations, water supply and sewage disposal systems, schools, hospitals, parks, cinemas, restaurants, and so on (Harvey, 2006, p.233). Capitalists investing in the secondary circuit (e.g., property development) are doing so in the expectation of realising their profits either in the form of rental income, or from the enhanced future sale price of the building. The *tertiary circuit* involves investment in science and technology, education and health care among others. Although usually undertaken by the state, investment in these latter areas may eventually improve the profitability of capital via increased productivity and improving labour capability (see Pacione, 2005, p.151).

The secondary and tertiary circuits are very different in character, but they share an important common feature. In both cases, there is a potentially considerable time lag between the time when investment is made and the time when profits are eventually realised. In other words, both these circuits have a capacity to absorb surplus value for a long time before releasing it back into circulation many years later. In other words, both these circuits have a temporal dimension and both may be part of what can be called a 'temporal fix' (a concept that will be examined below).

The other important point to note is that circuits of capital also have their spatial dimension. Indeed, capital switching may happen both within and between regions. Some regions may be engaged in specific circuits of capital and the crises of those circuits may be translated into regional crises. Capital switching thus may involve not only moving surpluses into secondary and tertiary circuits of capital within a given region, but also into various circuits outside the regional (or national) economy in question. One way or another, geography plays an important role in the operation of the capitalist system. Spatial structures (built environment) created around us (e.g., sub-urbanisation, shopping malls, office blocks) can be seen as being part of the circuits of capital. As such, they can also be part of the answer to the question of why capitalism has managed to avoid terminal collapse despite its inherent contradictions. This leads us to the concept of a 'spatial fix'.

UNEVEN DEVELOPMENT AND 'SPATIAL FIX'

Spatial fix, or more precisely, spatio-temporal fix is another concept developed by David Harvey (1982, 2006). The concept refers to the way in which both time and space play a central role in the operation (and survival) of the capitalist system. The word 'fix' has a double meaning here. On the one hand, it describes a situation in which a certain portion of capital is '*literally fixed in and on the land* in some physical form for a relatively long period of time' (Harvey, 2003, p.115; emphasis added). On the other hand, the term 'fix' is used as 'a metaphor for a *particular kind of solution to capitalist crises* through temporal deferral and geographical expansion' (ibid.; emphasis added).

Therefore, there are several ways in which capitalism can cope with crises (see Coe et al., 2007, pp.70–72, for a short summary):

- devaluation;
- macroeconomic management;
- temporal displacement of capital (temporal fix);
- spatial displacement of capital (spatial fix).

Devaluation (already mentioned in Chapter 3) may involve the devaluation of money (via inflation), devaluation of labour (via unemployment) as well as the devaluation of productive capacities (devaluation or physical destruction). *Macroeconomic management* involves attempts to bring together idle capital and idle labour (the unemployed) back into productive use through government intervention. This can be done by curbing excessive labour exploitation (which pushes up wages and increases the spending power of the population) or through increased government spending (to create jobs and stimulate demand), for instance. An example of such an approach to the economic crisis is Keynesianism, which we will discuss in more detail in Chapter 8. More generally. various modes of regulation may be instituted to prevent the system from collapsing (e.g., see the box on Regulation Theory in Coe et al., 2007, p.71). A *temporal displacement of capital* (*temporal fix*) involves placing surplus capital in long-term ventures. This may include the investment in secondary and tertiary circuits of capital discussed above. Social expenditures and long-term investments in infrastructure of various kinds are examples of this, as is the advancement of loans (credit). The effect of such temporal displacements of capital is that they avert crises at the present and delay them into the future. A temporal fix is therefore responsible for expanding the *time* horizons of the circuits of capital.

The *spatial displacement of capital* (*spatial fix*), on the other hand, expands the *spatial* horizons of the capitalist system. The spatial fix includes the opening of new spaces of production (e.g., those with cheaper production costs); spatial expansion into new markets (with the effect of boosting much-needed demand); finding new sources of raw materials; or the re-creation of old places (places previously devalued). The logic behind the spatial fix has been summarised by Harvey as follows:

> If the surpluses of capital and of labour power exist within a given territory (such as a nation-state or a region) and cannot be absorbed internally (either by geographical adjustments or social expenditures) then they must be sent elsewhere to find a fresh terrain for their profitable realization if they are not to be devalued. (Harvey, 2003, p.117)

In other words, capital constantly searches for the spaces in which surplus value can be created (see also the 'see-saw' theory of Neil Smith, 1984). This search for new spaces of capital accumulation may involve re-investment in previously devalued old spaces or pushing the boundaries of capitalist enterprise beyond the established circuits of capital. Understanding the operation of the economy in this light opens up new ways of looking at economic processes associated with globalisation (see more in Chapter 7). One way or another, it is important to note that

Harvey's conceptualisation of economic geographies include the notion that uneven development 'is not only an inevitable feature of capitalism, but also a *necessary* one' (Coe et al., 2007, p.66; original emphasis). This is because: '[s]pace is *not just the container* in which capitalism takes place. Rather, economic geography is *fundamental* and *inherent* to the successful operation of the system' (ibid., p.72; emphasis added). To put it differently, 'uneven development is both a *cause* and an *outcome* of capitalist growth' (ibid., p.84; emphasis added). Further insights into the issue of uneven development in the capitalist economy have been offered by the concept of spatial divisions of labour to which we now turn.

SPATIAL DIVISIONS OF LABOUR

The concept of spatial divisions of labour has been developed by a British geographer Doreen Massey in her highly influential book *Spatial Divisions of Labour: Social Structures and the Geography of Production* (Massey, 1984; with the second edition appearing a decade later – see Massey, 1995). In it, Massey has discussed the geography of production and uneven development through the prism of the *social relations of production*. Under capitalism, social relations of production revolve 'around the social relations between capital and labour, employers and employees, investors and wage earners. These are essentially relations of economic power, within which control lies with capital, employers, and investors' (Dicken and Lloyd, 1990, p.352).

Another way of putting this would be to say that social relations under capitalism are structured along the relations based on class (e.g., the capitalist class on the one hand, and the working class on the other). Massey's point is that social relations are also organised spatially and this is captured in her concept of spatial divisions of labour. In order to explain the concept of spatial divisions of labour, we will first examine two key related concepts – technical division of labour and social division of labour.

Technical division of labour, in its simplest form, involves the division of labour within a firm. As we have seen in the example of the pin-making factory (see Chapter 3), the process of making pins involves 18 distinct stages. The technical division of labour implies a division of the production process into distinctive tasks and the assignment of workers to these tasks. In the pin-making factory described by Adam Smith, ten workers covered 18 tasks (Figure 5.3). But it is possible to imagine that a more refined technical division of labour can be achieved if an additional eight workers were hired so that each worker specialises in one task.

Source: Background picture adapted from www.timesonline.co.uk/tol/news/uk/
article617514.ece.

Figure 5.3   Technical division of labour

Social division of labour, on the other hand, is a more general concept
that goes beyond the boundaries of a firm to describe the roles performed
by various people or groups of people within a society at large. Social divisions of labour thus may refer to the division of labour between various
sectors (e.g., agriculture, fisheries, pin-making, car-making industry,
banking sector, education sector, health service and so on) or to workers
in different jobs or professions (e.g., farmer, fisherman, pin-maker, car
factory worker, banker, teacher, nurse, etc.) (see also Coffey, 1996). One
way or another, the concept helps us to understand that we rely on each
other for society to function. In the capitalist society, however, both technical and social divisions of labour reflect the underlying capitalist social
relations of production (e.g., see Massey, 1995, pp.30–38).

The idea of spatial divisions of labour is based on the recognition that
the economy is characterised by complex technical and social divisions
of labour that are reflected in complex spatial structures. Massey argues
that the economy cannot work at the 'head of a pin' – therefore the
spatial dimension is always present (see also our discussion in Chapter 2).
Inevitably, *the economy is stretched over space and so are social relations
of production*. In other words, social relations are organised spatially. The
spatial organisation of the economy is rather complex, reflecting complex
spatial divisions of labour.

A simple example of the spatial division of labour involves the division
of labour within a firm, in which different tasks are undertaken in different

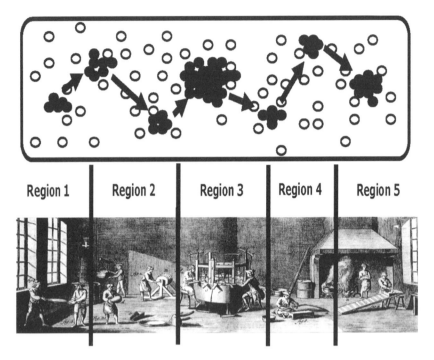

Region 1 Region 2 Region 3 Region 4 Region 5

Source: Illustration by Martin Sokol and background picture adapted from www.
timesonline.co.uk/tol/news/uk/article617514.ece.

Figure 5.4   Spatial division of labour

locations. For instance, head office functions, administrative functions, research and development (R&D) and production functions can all be located in different regions. Also it is possible to imagine a situation where the different stages of production are located in different regions (see Figure 5.4). Another example of the spatial division of labour involves the division of labour between firms and sectors – for example, the steel industry, the electronics industry, financial services) concentrating in certain locations (regions). One way or other, at the level of the national economy, all regions are functionally interconnected through economic linkages and social relations of production. Individual regions thus must be seen as parts of a wider economic structure. The economic power and fortunes of particular regions depend on their position within the wider social relations of production (i.e., on their position within the wider spatial divisions of labour). The position within the spatial divisions of labour, in turn, is modified or maintained by successive rounds of investment (see

Coe et al., 2007, pp.78–80). Uneven development, therefore, cannot be understood in relation to the characteristics of individual regions only. Rather it involves a recognition that *the roles the regions are playing are mutually constituted*. In addition, it involves a recognition that uneven development can vary not only in degree (i.e., the extent of disparities – the rate of unemployment, for instance) but also in character (qualitatively different regional problems; Mohan, 1999, pp.10–11). Simply put, high-level strategic control and R&D functions would remain concentrated in major metropolitan regions in core countries; management of operations would be delegated to regional capitals; while routine operations and production itself would be based in the periphery (see Hymer, 1972; Cohen et al., 1979; MacKinnon and Cumbers, 2007, pp.147–8 and Box 7.2 on p.148; see also Coe et al., 2007, pp.78–80).

Doreen Massey offers an example of London and the South-East of England which, she argues, 'was (and still is) the prime locus of control, of strategic planning, of finance, of the resources for research and innovation' (Massey, 1995, p.3). Because of the social relations involved, the South-East of England is, Massey argues, 'in a position of structural dominance in comparison with, *and in relation to*, other regions of the country' (ibid.; original emphasis). Many of the other regions of the country, meanwhile, remained dominated by branch plant manufacturing, simple line assembly or other, subordinate tasks.

Thus, Massey insists, this is not about the geography of jobs, but rather the geography 'of power relations, of dominance and subordination, of enablement and influence, and of symbols and signification' (ibid.). Massey is well aware that the power relations of 'dominance and subordination' are not confined to the national space. Rather, the spatial divisions of labour within a national economy are embedded within a wider international context of economic and social relations. Simply put, national economies are themselves part of much wider *international divisions of labour* and power relations that such a division of labour entails (see also Chapter 7). The significance of the international divisions of labour has been growing hand in hand with the processes of globalisation (e.g., Coffey, 1996). The way in which regional economies (and whole nations) are economically interdependent on each other is also reflected in the concept of the core-periphery model to which we now turn.

CORE-PERIPHERY

The key idea of the *core-periphery model* is that uneven development results from a set of uneven economic relations between a (dominant)

Unequal exchange of values

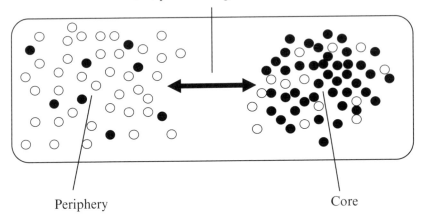

Periphery   Core

Source: Illustration by Martin Sokol.

Figure 5.5   *Core-periphery*

core region and (dominated) periphery regions. Simply put, economically advanced regions (or national economies) become rich by exploiting
economically less developed regions (or nations). The idea of domination
and subordination between regions has a strong resonance with the principle of exploitation of labour under capitalism (although not all core-
periphery concepts are necessarily Marxist; see Gill and Law, 1988, p.54
or Krugman, 1991, and the discussion above on cumulative causation).
According to the Marxist-inspired core-periphery models the economic
fortunes of regions are dependent on their economic power within the
uneven economic relations that allow for an unequal exchange (of values)
to take place between regions (Figure 5.5). Unequal exchange, in turn,
contributes towards uneven development between regions (see Coe et
al., 2007, pp.82–4). The insistence by the core-periphery model that the
fortunes of regions are mutually linked thus echoes both the concepts of
spatial divisions of labour reviewed above and that of cumulative causation introduced in the first section of this chapter.

The core-periphery model offers a simple way of looking at economic
dependency between economies and has been applied at various spatial
scales from national to international and global. For instance, the above-
mentioned South-East of England may be seen as a core region of the
UK national economy. In relation to this, the extent to which Britain is
economically divided into prosperous South and declining North by the

North–South divide has been debated (see Chapter 1; and Mohan, 1999, pp.3–9). Meanwhile, at the European level, the South-East of England can be seen as but a part of a much larger core area that stretches from London through Germany to Northern Italy (e.g., see Dicken, 2003, p.77; 2007, p.65). With the fall of state-socialism in Central and Eastern Europe, the extent to which the East–West development divide characterises the New Europe has become an issue (e.g., see Sokol, 2001). Finally, at the global level, reference is frequently made to the advanced 'core economies' of the Global North (a group of countries including the US, Canada, UK, France, Germany, etc.) and the extent to which the global North–South divide is a useful way of describing divisions within the global economy (see also Chapter 1). While the core-periphery model has its limits (for instance, it hides inequalities within both the core and peripheral regions), it nevertheless alerts us to some important issues about the mutual interdependencies within and between economies and the creation of 'core' and 'peripheral' spaces at various spatial scales (please note that *economic* peripherality is not necessarily the same as *geographical* peripherality).

CONCLUSION

This chapter has examined economic geography concepts that have been inspired by Marxist thought. Collectively, these concepts emphasise the point that uneven development is an inherent and unavoidable feature of the capitalist economy based on exploitative social relations (stretched over space) and that uneven development is both the cause and outcome of capitalist economic growth. In addition to this, it could be argued that Marxist economic geographers made an important contribution to the big questions about how the capitalist economy itself functions. The concept of 'spatial fix' in particular offers insights into the questions as to why and how capitalism survived until now and what role geography plays in overcoming the contradictions of capitalist accumulation. From the Marxist perspective then, economic globalisation can be seen as an incessant search for profitable spaces for the absorption of the surplus value. In this way, not only spatial horizons of the ever-expanding capitalist system are being pushed further, but a crisis is being pushed away in both time and space. Yet, according to Marxists, internal contradictions of capitalism cannot be resolved, and crises can only be delayed, but not avoided. The most recent global financial and economic crisis is perhaps a good reminder of this.

FURTHER READING

Coe, N.M., P.F. Kelly and H.W.C. Yeung (2007) *Economic Geography: A Contemporary Introduction.* (Oxford: Blackwell) Chapter 3.
Dicken, P. and P. Lloyd (1990) *Location in Space: Theoretical Perspectives in Economic Geography.* (New York: Harper Collins Publishers). Chapters 9 and 10.
Hudson, R. (2005) *Economic Geographies: Circuits, Flows and Spaces.* (London: Sage).
MacKinnon, D. and A. Cumbers (2007) *An Introduction to Economic Geography: Globalization, Uneven Development and Place.* (Harlow: Pearson/Prentice Hall) Chapter 3.

More advanced readers may want to read the following classic works of Harvey and Massey
Harvey, D. (2006) *The Limits to Capital* (new and fully updated edition). (London and New York: Verso).
Massey, D. (1995) *Spatial Divisions of Labour: Social Structures and the Geography of Production* (second edition). (London: Macmillan).

USEFUL WEBSITES*

http://davidharvey.org/ – a website of David Harvey, a Distinguished Professor at the City University of New York (CUNY), containing video lectures explaining the fundamentals of the Marxist theory.
http://www.youtube.com/watch?v=qOP2V_np2c0 – animated lecture of David Harvey on 'Crises of Capitalism' available on YouTube (produced by RSA Animate).

* Both accessed 2 March 2011.

6.   Alternative approaches and new economic geography

INTRODUCTION

This chapter will examine concepts and theories associated with various alternative approaches to economies and their geographies. In doing so, the chapter will provide basic insights into concepts associated with *new economic geography*. Many (although not all) of these concepts have been developed from intellectual vibrations of the evolutionary-institutionalist perspective, which has been introduced in Chapter 3. Owning to these foundations, new economic geography approaches often provide a stark contrast to both the neo-classical and Marxist approaches in the way they conceptualise the operation of economies over space. Indeed, by taking on board various social, cultural, institutional and other factors, new economic geography approaches are shedding a new light on the issue of uneven development. This is a vibrant area of geography and one that has seen many exciting developments in recent years. Having said that, it is important to recognise that some of the new concepts are still hotly debated. Also, you need to be aware that many scholars use a combination of various approaches in their study of economic geographies. Therefore, a sharp delineation of boundaries between various perspectives is sometimes not easy. However, some key differences between the neo-classical and Marxist approaches on the one hand, and new economic geography and other alternative approaches on the other hand, are apparent and will be highlighted in this chapter.

   The chapter will begin by discussing geographical implications of broad sectoral shifts between agriculture, manufacturing and services (stages theory); product and industry life cycles (cycle theories); technological shifts (wave theories); and post-Fordism. This will set a stage for the examination of selected new economic geography concepts. The chapter will specifically focus on the emergence of knowledge-based and learning economies in the form of regional innovation systems, clusters and learning regions. In relation to this, the chapter will also discuss the role of networks, trust and social capital in regional economic development. Finally, the chapter will examine the notions of culture, ethnicity and gender and their relevance for the conceptualisation of uneven development and their role in economies more generally.

STAGE, CYCLES AND WAVE THEORIES, TECHNICAL CHANGE AND POST-FORDISM

Stages Theory: Agriculture, Manufacturing and Services

Stages theory is the first of a group of theories that look upon economic development as 'historical and evolutionary processes' (Pike et al., 2006, p.78). The starting point of the stages theory is a recognition that the economy is composed of four major sectors:

- primary sector (agriculture and extractive activities);
- secondary sector (manufacturing);
- tertiary sector (services);
- quaternary sector (research and knowledge-intensive activities).

Statistical offices around the world are routinely using the split of economic activities into these major sectors to capture the economic structure of national and regional economies. The key idea of the stages theory is that as societies and economies develop, they move (evolve) through 'stages' of economic growth from agriculture to manufacture to services to knowledge-based forms of development (ibid.), each representing a more advanced stage of development. There is therefore a strong evolutionary logic behind this kind of conceptualisation, as if the economy was evolving from the most primitive to the most sophisticated forms (echoing modern thinking about biological evolution).

To a large extent, the sectoral shifts from primary to secondary to tertiary and quaternary activities can indeed be observed in the real world. The importance of each of the sectors changes over time, and this can be measured both in terms of the share of employment and the relative importance of these sectors in the economic output (GDP) of a given economy. Advanced economies are said to be characterised by a very small agricultural sector, continuously declining manufacturing sector, large and expanding service sector and, more recently, growing quaternary sector. The growth of the tertiary and quaternary sectors, in turn, fuels the views that advanced economies are in fact entering a stage of the knowledge-based economy (see more below). Seen in this light, uneven development can be considered as a consequence of the unevenness in development stages between various regions (or whole nations). However, things are probably more complicated than that. As we have seen in the previous chapter, regions (and nations) are functionally interdependent and their roles may be determined by their position within the wider spatial divisions of labour (see also Chapter 7).

Cycle Theories: Products and Profits

Cycle theories are also concerned with the process of economic evolution. However, they focus on the stages of development (life cycles) of individual products or industries. In its simplest version, the *product life cycle theory* suggests that products progress through various stages of development – from a product's introduction to growth to maturity to saturation and decline (see Dicken, 2003, pp.104–5; 2007, pp.93–4; Pike et al., 2006, pp.79–80). Each stage of the product life cycle is associated with different locational patterns (geographies). The conception of a new product, for example, can result from an innovation, the original location of which can be a historical accident (although it is likely that innovative firms introducing new products are located close to key supplier and research and development (R&D) facilities usually found in the core regions). As the product matures and the market for it expands, however, there is a scope for mass production to be moved to less developed regions where cheaper labour can be found. A more sophisticated version of the product life cycle theory is a *profit cycle theory*, which focuses on the product's profit stages and associated locational patterns (see more in Pike et al., 2006, pp.79–82).

Wave Theories, Technical Change and Post-Fordism

Wave theories (or theories of *long-waves*) are based on the idea that economic growth occurs in a series of 50-year long-waves (see Dicken, 2003, pp.87–9; 2007, pp.75–7; Pike et al., 2006, pp.82–3; Coe et al., 2007, pp.123–5). Such long-waves are also known as *Kondratiev waves* (or Kondratiev cycles) after the Russian economist who first identified them (Knox and Agnew, 1998, p.12). Each Kondratiev wave (or K-wave) may be divided into four phases: prosperity, recession, depression and recovery. Importantly, each wave is associated with 'particularly significant technological changes around which other innovations – in production, distribution and organization – cluster and ultimately spread through the economy' (Dicken, 2003, p.87). In other words, each wave is underpinned by a progressively more advanced *techno-economic paradigm* (Pike et al., 2006, p.82). So far, five Kondratiev waves have been identified, each underpinned by a specific set of technologies and type of industries and associated with particular locations (regions and nations) in which these industries flourished (before fading away and passing an opportunity to new locations to growth in a subsequent wave).

The first Kondratiev wave is sometimes referred to as the 'early mechanisation' wave (see Dicken, 2003, p.88; 2007, p.76; Coe et al., 2007, Figure 5.2 on p.124). Lasting from about the 1780s through to the 1830s and being mostly associated with regions in Britain, France and Belgium, the first wave was associated with textile industries, iron working/casting and water power. The subsequent second Kondratiev wave, of 'steam power and railway' (1840s to 1880s) was based on steam engine technologies, steamships, machine tools, iron and steel industries and railway equipment. Among the regions associated with the second wave are: Britain (South Wales, North-East England, Central Scotland), Germany (Ruhr), France, Belgium and the US (see also Pike et al., 2006, pp.82–3). The third wave of 'electrical and heavy engineering' (1890s–1940s), was associated with electric power and the emergence of electrical engineering, electrical machinery, heavy engineering and armaments, heavy chemicals and synthetic dyestuffs. The spatial core of the third Kondratiev wave included regions in Germany (e.g., Hessen), the US, Britain (e.g., West Midlands or Greater London), France, Belgium, Netherlands and Switzerland. The fourth wave coincided with the post-war boom years (late 1940s–70s) and is known as the *Fordist mass production* Kondratiev wave. The main industrial branches that were associated with this wave included: automobiles, trucks, tractors, tanks, aircraft, consumer durables, process plant, synthetic materials and petrochemicals. The Fordist mass production wave was led by the US, Germany, Switzerland, Sweden and other European countries, Japan, Canada and Australia (e.g., Dicken, 2003, p.88).

Finally, it has been argued that we are now in the midst of the fifth Kondratiev wave (from about the 1970s onwards). This is based mostly on computers, digital information technology, the Internet, software, telecommunication, optical fibres, robotics and biotechnology. It is often referred to as the *post-Fordist* wave or the 'information and communication' wave, not least because information and communication technology (ICT) is considered as a key technology (ibid., p.89). Again, there are specific geographical locations associated with this current technological wave. However, apart from the 'core' economies (US, Europe and Japan), 'emerging' economies like Taiwan and Korea are also claimed to be part of this wave (see Dicken, 2007, p.76). Silicon Valley, in the US, has often been portrayed as the most successful example of a regional economy of the new post-Fordist wave. More recently, Silicon Valley has also been described as the best example of a successful regional innovation system, high-tech cluster or a learning region – concepts that will be examined in turn (see also Box 6.1).

BOX 6.1   SILICON VALLEY

Silicon Valley, in California, is seen as an exemplary centre of innovation and symbol of economic success and technological superiority of the US. Specialising in electronics and ICTs, and employing about 400,000 people in high-tech companies, this iconic region is considered to be the biggest and the most successful concentration of ICT firms in the world. Originally centred on Santa Clara county and now spreading around the entire San Francisco Bay, it was once 'famous primarily for its apricot and walnut orchards' (Saxenian, 1996, p.11). A spectacular transformation, from a predominantly agricultural region back in the late 1940s, into a leading technology region within a space of a couple of decades, has been capturing the imagination of policy-makers, business leaders and academics alike.

From a theoretical viewpoint, the phenomenon of Silicon Valley can be described and understood in a number of ways. From a mainstream economic perspective, the region can be seen as a successful *agglomeration*, originally established with a handful of small electronic firms, and subsequently growing thanks to self-reinforcing effects of *circular and cumulative causation* (concepts discussed in Chapter 4). From a Marxist perspective, the emergence of Silicon Valley can be seen as an example of *capital switching* – from old declining industries (and locations) towards new industries (and locations) that carry a promise of higher rates of profit (see Chapter 5). From an evolutionary perspective, the Valley can be understood as a spatial expression of new product or industry cycle, involving new 'sunrise' industries. Equally, it can be seen as an example of a shift towards a *new techno-economic paradigm* or as a spatial expression of the fifth Kondratiev, post-Fordist, 'information and communication' wave. Alternatively, Silicon Valley can be understood as being part of a major shift from an industrial economy towards a new post-industrial, *knowledge-based economy*, accompanied by a geographical shift of economic activity away from old manufacturing 'rustbelt' regions (traditionally concentrated on the East Coast of the US) towards new 'sunbelt' regions (including the West Coast). Meanwhile, from the point of view of new economic geography, Silicon Valley can be described as a *regional innovation system*, *cluster* or *learning region* (see this chapter).

Seen through the prism of new economic geography, the
success of regions such as Silicon Valley needs to be appreciated
in the light of local and regional factors, such as specific regional
cultures. Perhaps the most vivid description of Silicon Valley in
this light has been offered by Annalee Saxenian (1996) in her
highly influential book *Regional Advantage*. Saxenian argued that
the ascendance of Silicon Valley can only be explained if one
looks at the cultural traits that distinguish it from other regions.
She famously contrasted Silicon Valley with Route 128, a high-
technology corridor around Boston, Massachusetts on the East
Coast of the US. She argued that differences between the two
regions went well beyond the superficial disparities between 'laid
back' California and the more 'buttoned up' East Coast (Saxenian,
1996, p.2). She argued that (despite similar high-technology
base) the two regions represented two contrasting cases of
regional industrial organisation. In her view, the Route 128 region
was dominated by a small number of big, inward-looking corporations, overly dependent on government contracts – all of which
meant that Route 128 was losing out to, and eventually was over-
taken by, Silicon Valley. By contrast, the dynamism of Silicon
Valley apparently resulted from a regional network-based industrial system (made of a large number of small companies) that
'promotes collective learning and flexible adjustment among specialist producers of a complex of related technologies' (ibid.). In
Silicon Valley, she argues:

companies compete intensely while at the same time learning from one
another about changing markets and technologies through informal communication and collaborative practices; and loosely linked team structures encourage horizontal communication among firm divisions and
with outside suppliers and customers. The functional boundaries within
firms are porous in a network system, as are the boundaries between
firms themselves and between firms and local institutions such as trade
associations and universities. (Ibid., pp.2–3)

In contrast, the Route 128 region was characterised by a
'regional culture that encourages stability and self-reliance' (in part
reflecting Puritan traditions of Boston) and where corporate hierarchies ensure 'that authority remains centralized and information
tends to flow vertically' (ibid., p.2). She concluded that the 'contrasting experiences of Silicon Valley and Route 128 suggest that

industrial systems built on regional networks are more flexible and technologically dynamic than those in which experimentation and learning are confined to individual firms' (ibid., p.161) while adding that 'Silicon Valley continues to reinvent itself as its specialized producers learn collectively and adjust to one another's needs through shifting patterns of competition and collaboration' (ibid.).

For Saxenian, spatial clustering alone 'does not create mutually beneficial interdependencies' because an industrial system 'may be geographically agglomerated and yet have limited capacity for adaptation' (ibid.). Nevertheless, she argued that '[g]eographical proximity promotes the repeated interaction and mutual trust needed to sustain collaboration' (ibid.). Consequently, and paradoxically, 'regions offer an important source of competitive advantage even as production and markets become increasingly global' (ibid.).

The work of Saxenian has had a massive influence on the way new economic geography conceptualises regional economic development. Key features of her approach are reflected in the much celebrated notions of networks, culture, trust, competition *and* collaboration, regional institutions, collective learning or untraded interdependencies – all of which are discussed in this chapter. However, it is important to underline that all of these concepts, and their role in economic development, continue to be debated. The reality of Silicon Valley itself is perhaps less glamorous than many optimistic accounts would suggest. Importantly, the purported success of Silicon Valley cannot be simply reduced to local or regional factors. Indeed, the unparalleled growth of the Valley was in part underpinned by the federal government through multi-billion defence and space contracts (openly acknowledged, but still downplayed, by Saxenian), especially during the Cold War. Silicon Valley thus can be seen as part of a government-sponsored 'gunbelt' (Markusen et al., 1991) in the West Coast of the US. Second, despite the economic success, not everybody got rich and Silicon Valley is characterised by significant social and spatial inequality (e.g., see Pike et al., 2006, pp.217–19). Finally, while Silicon Valley has shown a great deal of economic resilience, it is by no means immune from economic downturns and crises, including the most recent one.

TOWARDS A NEW ECONOMIC GEOGRAPHY

This section will examine more closely concepts that are associated with the new economic geography. As already discussed earlier in the book, there are two types of 'new economic geographies'. One is associated with the work of geographers as part of the cultural turn, the other with the work of economists such as Krugman, building on neo-classical location theory (see Box 2.1 in Chapter 2). This section refers to the former. It will start by discussing regional innovation systems and clusters, move on to examine learning regions and finally look at notions of networks, trust, social capital and culture and their relevance for economic geographies.

Regional Innovation Systems and Clusters

While the concepts such as techno-economic paradigm, post-Fordism and the long-waves of development continue to be debated, they are nevertheless useful in that they highlight the importance of the link between economic development and technology. More specifically, they make the point that economic growth is dependent on either the technological innovation (i.e., the development of brand new technologies) or the adoption of new technologies (developed elsewhere).

In terms of the technological innovation, the literature distinguishes between two basic models: the linear innovation model and the interactive innovation model. The *linear* innovation model involves the linear stage of innovation from: (1) idea/invention, to (2) design and development of prototypes; (3) production; and finally (4) sale. The *interactive* innovation model, on the other hand, recognises that innovation is an interactive social process and cannot be reduced to a one-way linear process. Instead, the interactive innovation model emphasises mutual (two-way) interactions between various stages of innovation and between producers and users (customers). The concept of the interactive innovation model has been influenced by evolutionary and institutional approaches (discussed in Chapter 3). Originally, it has been applied at the national level in the form of the *national innovation systems* model (e.g., Lundvall, 1992; Lundvall and Maskell, 2003).

However, economic geographers quickly pointed out that the kinds of interactions implied in the national innovation systems model are probably best achieved at the regional level. In other words, geography, once again, matters. Indeed, it has been argued that within the regional context, interactions between individual firms (suppliers, collaborators as well as competitors), firms and public R&D laboratories, firms and universities, and firms and their customers may benefit from close geographical proximity and evolve into *regional innovation systems* (Braczyk et al., 1998). There are a large number of similar concepts that try to describe the phenomenon of innovative regions. Such concepts include:

- *innovative milieus* (Aydalot and Keeble, 1988; Camagni, 1991);
- *technopoles* (Castells and Hall, 1994);
- *high-technology districts* (e.g., Keeble, 1989, 1992);
- *flexible specialisation districts* (Piore and Sabel, 1984);
- *new industrial districts* (Amin and Thrift, 1992);
- *new industrial spaces* (Scott, 1988);
- *sunbelt regions* (Hall and Markusen, 1985);
- *intelligent regions* (Cooke and Morgan, 1994).

More recently, the concepts of clusters and learning regions have gained considerable currency among academics and policy-makers alike. It is therefore worth examining both these concepts in a bit more detail. We will first start by discussing the concept of clusters before examining learning regions in the subsequent sub-section.

Clusters have been defined as the 'geographic concentration of inter-connected companies, specialised suppliers and service providers, firms in related industries, and associated institutions (e.g., universities, standards agencies, and trade associations) in particular fields that compete but also cooperate' (Porter, 2000, p.253; cited in Pike et al., 2006, p.110). The notion of the 'geographic concentration' evokes the concept of *agglomeration* (discussed in Chapter 4). Indeed, the two terms (clusters and agglomerations) are often used interchangeably (e.g., see Coe et al., 2007, pp.143–5). However, one could argue that there are a small number of important differences between the two concepts. Two such differences will be highlighted here.

First, it is important to notice that the above definition provided by Porter already signals one important feature of clusters, which clearly distinguishes them from agglomerations: while the neo-classical approach emphasises competition between firms as the key economic driver, the concept of clusters recognises that interactions between various economic agents may involve the elements of both competition *and* cooperation (see also Scott, 1988). Moreover, some would argue that the element of active cooperation may not only apply to economic agents such as firms, trade associations and universities, but also to actors such as trade unions and local and regional government. A term *associational economy* (Amin and Thrift, 1995a; Cooke and Morgan, 1998) has been coined to capture this cooperative nature among principal economic players. This is an important point, because it implies that the contradictions between capital and labour (see Chapter 3 for a discussion of the Marxist approach to the economy) can somehow be overcome. Indeed, it has been argued that, in successful regions, *cooperative* institutional arrangements exist to coordinate the actions of regional players. This also represents another important contrast to the neo-classical framework, which sees the 'invisible hand' of the market as the key mechanism for guiding the actions of economic agents (see Chapter 3). The ability of institutional arrangements to guide collective action in successful regions has been referred to as *institutional thickness* (Amin and Thrift, 1994, p.14). Institutional thickness arises from coordination between a plethora of regional institutions, which include firms, financial institutions, local chambers of commerce, training agencies, trade associations, local authorities, development agencies, innovation centres, clerical bodies, marketing boards, government agencies and trade unions.

Another important difference between agglomerations and clusters lies in a *type* of interaction between various regional players. As mentioned in Chapter 3, both neo-classical and Marxist approaches focus on formal market transactions. Formal market transactions are transactions that have a price tag attached to them. Such transactions are also called *traded interdependencies*; that is, formal trading relationships between economic agents (see Coe et al., 2007, pp.137–9). An example of a formal market transaction or a traded interdependency includes a formal contract between a supplier and a client (or, as we have seen in Chapter 4, between a pin-making firm and a specialised accountancy practice). Firms may also use formal contracts to regulate relationships in joint cooperative projects, for instance. It is these traded transactions that form an agglomeration in the neo-classical, strictly economic, sense (as discussed in Chapter 4).

However, as already mentioned in Chapter 3, the economy cannot be reduced to market transactions only. Indeed, in addition to traded interdependencies, regional economies are made up of a vast array of exchanges that are not based on formal market relationships. Such non-market exchanges are also called *untraded interdependencies* (Storper, 1997; see Coe et al., 2007, pp.139–43). These are less tangible, but not less important, interactions between economic agents. Examples of such interactions include informal information exchanges (e.g., about emerging technologies and markets) and various forms of cooperation happening through informal networks and interpersonal contacts (rather than formal contracts). Often, such exchanges are based on trust and reciprocity, and are lubricated by a shared culture (see more below). What emerges from this process are so-called *relational assets*, which are not based on economic, but primarily on social and cultural factors. This then, constitutes the second major difference between a cluster and a (narrowly defined) economic agglomeration. In other words, cluster is perhaps much closer to Alfred Marshall's century-old concept of 'industrial districts'. Indeed, contemporary innovative regions have been described as 'neo-Marshallian nodes in global networks' (Amin and Thrift, 1992). It has been argued that in successful regions, untraded interdependencies foster technology spillovers, innovation, learning and ultimately competitiveness of the firms involved and of the entire regional economy. However, the reality is perhaps more complex (and confusing) and the ability of the cluster concept to explain regional economic success has been questioned. Indeed, despite the fact that cluster is one of the most celebrated concepts in new economic geography, important criticisms have been levied upon it (e.g., Martin and Sunley, 2003).

Knowledge Economies and Learning Regions

Learning region is another influential concept that aims to account for dynamic innovative regions (Pike et al., 2006, pp.97–102; Coe et al., 2007, p.341). However, unlike the regional innovation system and (to a lesser extent) cluster, the concept of the learning region focuses less on *technological* innovation. Instead, it emphasises the importance of 'learning' – that is, innovation as a wider social and economic process. From this point of view, the learning region can be seen as a regional dimension of the knowledge-based, learning economy (which we discussed in Chapter 3). In the definition provided by Richard Florida, learning regions 'function as collectors and repositories of knowledge and ideas, and provide the underlying environment and infrastructure which facilitates the flow of knowledge, ideas and learning' (Florida, 1995, p.257). The process of learning is defined very broadly here and goes beyond the usual meaning of individual learning (i.e., a formation of human capital). Instead, in line with the view that learning is a social process, the notion of learning encompasses a range of situations. Various versions of the learning region concept exist (e.g., Florida, 1995; Asheim, 1996; Morgan, 1997; see also Storper, 1997; Maskell et al., 1998; Lagendijk, 2000) and we have no space to review them all here. However, it could be argued that learning region theorists build on several commonly held positions. These positions could be tentatively summarised as follows (Sokol, 2003):

1. There is a commonly shared conviction that the role of *knowledge* in the economy and society is indeed growing (Florida, 1995; Maskell et al., 1998, p.3 and p.24; Amin and Thrift, 1999, p.293; see also Bryson et al., 2000) and that the current economy is best described as

the 'learning economy', 'knowledge economy' or 'knowledge-based economy' (e.g., Florida, 1995; Cooke, 2002; inter alia). Within such an economy (echoing Lundvall and Johnson, 1994), knowledge is considered as 'the most important resource and learning the most important process' (e.g., Morgan, 1998, p.230; Boekema et al., 2000). Consequently, '[k]nowledge has become a central organising concept for those concerned with regional economic development' and '*learning* has become the best way to understand regional economic change' (Malecki, 2000, p.119; original emphasis). In effect, the region has become conceptualised as a 'nexus of learning processes' (Cooke and Morgan, 1998).

2. It is maintained that learning is a *collective* process (e.g., Asheim, 1996). Therefore, it is not confined to individuals, or even individual firms, rather it is conceptualised as occurring between firms (producers, suppliers, competitors); between firms and consumers (users); and between firms and a plethora of local or regional institutions (Amin and Thrift, 1994; Morgan, 1997; Storper, 1997).

3. The result of this learning process, that is, knowledge, is, however, a rather 'leaky phenomenon' (Storper and Scott, 1995, p.510). Indeed, as soon as it is codified, the global knowledge economy renders knowledge ubiquitous and makes it open to competitors' appropriation and replication. Therefore, it has been argued, it is *non-codified* or *tacit* knowledge that is a crucial source of competitive advantage (Storper, 1995; Maskell et al., 1998; Maskell and Malmberg, 1999).

4. Tacit knowledge requires regular face-to-face contact between involved actors. It is assumed that in the absence of 'magic carpets' (Storper and Scott, 1995, p.506) these face-to-face relations are only sustainable within a certain spatial (geographical) proximity (see also Cooke and Morgan, 1998).

5. Besides, what is needed for successful 'collective learning' is a set of *informal* institutions such as habits, conventions, rules of conduct, lubricated by cooperative culture and trust (Storper, 1997; Cooke, 1998; Maskell et al., 1998; Maskell and Malmberg, 1999). These factors, it is believed, are place-specific and supported by regionally-based *formal* institutions that facilitate the exchange of knowledge and ideas between regional actors, guarantee continuous innovation and ensure coordination of regional action for the benefit of all participants (Amin and Thrift, 1994, 1999; Amin, 1999; Storper and Scott, 1995; Storper, 1997, 1999; Cooke and Morgan, 1998; inter alia). Thanks to 'localised learning' and 'institutional endowments' (Maskell et al., 1998, p.97), learning regions can thrive in the 'global knowledge economy', while becoming the basic organisational units

of such an economy (Florida, 1995; see also Storper and Scott, 1995; Storper, 1997, 1999).

To conclude, it could be said that in comparison to economics-based approaches, the above conceptualisation of learning regions brings very different answers to the questions of economic agglomeration and competitiveness. As Peter Maskell and his colleagues assert, 'it has to do with *knowledge creation* and with the development of *localised capabilities* that promote the learning process' (Maskell et al., 1998, p.193; original emphasis). Learning, knowledge creation and localised capabilities are believed to lie behind the success of advanced regions, such as Silicon Valley (Box 6.1; see also Pike et al., 2006, pp.212–19 and Coe et al., 2007, pp.144–5 for a discussion on Silicon Valley). What is more, some commentators believe that less-favoured regions can emulate the success of advanced regions by mimicking their institutional structures and creating favourable conditions for learning. In other words, it is believed that the new knowledge era offers opportunities to eradicate/overcome uneven development. However, it needs to be noted that the concept of the learning region and its ability to act as a catalyst for a more balanced development has been debated (e.g., see Hudson, 1999; Lovering, 1999; MacKinnon et al., 2002; Sokol, 2003; inter alia).

Networks, Trust and Social Capital

As we can see from the above, new economic geography approaches such as regional innovation systems, clusters and learning regions, differ substantially from both the neo-classical and conventional Marxist perspectives on economies and their geographies. Indeed, the notions of networks, trust and social capital help to shed a new light on the way regional economies work. The focus on networks is important, because they are seen as intermediate and institutionalised forms of social organisation that are neither markets nor (organisational) hierarchies. Instead, networks are seen as cooperative and reciprocal, especially when they are lubricated with mutual trust and shared culture (see also below). What emerges from such trustful relations and networks is *social capital*. Social capital can be defined as 'the associations, activities, or relations that bind people together as a community via certain norms and psychological capacities, notably trust, which are essential for civil society and productive of future collective action or goods, in the manner of other forms of capital' (Farr, 2004, pp.8–9; cited in Pike et al., 2006, p.92). Social capital is thus seen as an 'asset' for regional economies (see also the concept of 'relational assets' discussed above), an asset that neither neo-classical models, nor conventional Marxist approaches have captured. The new economic geography thus provides us with further insights into the ways economies and their geographies work. However, some key concepts and assumptions continue to be debated. This includes the notion of culture to which we now turn.

Culture, Ethnicity and Gender

Culture has become one of the key buzzwords of the new economic geography, in part reflecting the 'cultural turn' (Lee and Wills, 1997) in geography and in social sciences more widely. This area of geography has recently seen dramatic developments. In many ways, approaches that take culture seriously (and put it at the centre of attention) challenge the very notion of 'the economic' (see also discussion in Chapter 3). Indeed, the boundaries and the relations between 'the economy' and 'culture' are being questioned and problematised. The mutual constitution of 'the economic' and 'the cultural' is being emphasised. The terms such as 'cultural economies' and 'economic cultures' have been used to highlight this interconnection. More generally, it could be argued that these 'cultural' approaches destabilise the conventional notion of the economy (see also Chapter 2 for a discussion). Yet, many questions remain unanswered. Indeed, culture risks becoming a 'dustbin category' in economic geography 'for anything one cannot explain' (James, 2005, p.1199). Much remains to be done to elucidate the ways in which culture impacts on economic development, although many exciting insights have already been made (e.g., see Box 6.2).

Finally, it is worth highlighting that alongside the notion of culture, new economic geography has also paid increasing attention to the role of *ethnicity* and *gender* in economic processes. Again, this can be seen as an important diversion from and contrast to both Marxist approaches (that consider *class* as the most important category) and neo-classical theories (that largely disregard such categories altogether). Yet, both gender and ethnicity clearly play an important role in the economy – by influencing the way in which division of labour is organised, for example. Indeed, certain types of jobs display strong gender dimensions (e.g., male-dominated or female-dominated jobs) or particular types of jobs are being done by particular ethnic groups. Coe et al. (2007, Chapter 13) for example, provide an excellent account of ethnic economies in Toronto. Equally, ethnic dimension has been found important in migrant divisions of labour in London's low-pay jobs (see May et al., 2007; Wills et al., 2009; see also Box 1.2 in Chapter 1).

BOX 6.2   CULTURE AND HIGH-TECH REGIONAL CLUSTER OF UTAH, US

The notion of culture has attracted significant attention within new economic geography in recent years, but it is clear that much more needs to be done. Al James (2005) has highlighted an apparent paradox here, specifically focusing on the study of innovative regional economies. Indeed, while there appears to be a 'growing consensus that culture plays an important role in shaping the conditions conducive to innovation' (James, 2005, p.1212), culture remains 'inadequately conceptualized, theorized and empirically verified' (ibid., p.1213). This means that 'the precise impact of regional culture on the competitive performance of firms in innovative regional economies has yet to be fully specified, let alone measured' (ibid., p.1212). In his influential study of Utah's high-technology cluster, James (2005) set himself a task of identifying mechanisms through which regional culture is translated into corporate culture, in turn impacting on the innovation capacity of local firms and thus their ability to compete.

Literature on innovative regions distinguishes several important features that are said to promote innovation (ibid., p.1210, Table 6). These include *interfirm networks*, which promote, for example, information exchange between firms, allow information recombination and exploitation of overlapping technical knowledge. In other words, networks can promote collective learning. Interfirm linkages also allow the *exploitation of other firms' competences*, which can help firms to share resources (and thus reduce costs and risks), to gain new competence, to reduce time needed to market products and to facilitate group problem-solving via unexpected synergies. Another important ingredient is the involvement of *venture capital*, allowing firms, among others, to accelerate innovation and growth. Finally, successful regions are said to have a culture of accepting large workloads in short periods of calendar time and long or abnormal working hours – sometimes also called a 'sleeping bag under the desk' phenomenon. Equally, successful regions are claimed to have a rich 'afterwork socialising' culture, which blurs work and social identities, promotes informal information networks, helps diffuse tacit knowledge and reinforces existing formal corporate interactions and learning (see also Box 6.1).

Utah is uniquely positioned for a study of regional culture and its impact on regional innovation and economic competitiveness. A high-tech cluster has emerged there, benefiting from defence industry build-up during the 1960s, from the growth of software industry and services in the 1980s (in part helped by the relocation of various operations from Silicon Valley) and finally through a wave of start-up companies in the 1990s (ibid., p.1200). In the year 2000, Utah's Wasatch Front (including Salt Lake City and three other counties) boasted 2,100 high-tech firms, employing over 70,000 people. Out of many high-tech sectors present in Utah, the computer software sector, 'one of the defining industries of the knowledge economy' (ibid.) was the biggest in terms of number of firms (1,400), employment (23,000 people) and contribution to the economy (US$1.4bn or 45 per cent of the state's total high-tech payroll).

What makes Utah a particularly suitable case study is the fact that the regional economy is embedded in a strong and distinctive regional culture associated with the Mormon Church (also known as The Church of Jesus Christ of Latter-day Saints). Indeed, Mormons account for 75 per cent of the population of Utah and many of the software firms are either Mormon-owned and managed, or have a majority Mormon workforce, or both. Importantly, Mormonism is 'more than simply a creedal faith, it is a whole way of life requiring an almost total commitment in customs, values and lifestyle' (ibid.). Mormon culture includes prohibitions against alcohol and drug use, a commitment to fasting and prayer, modesty in dress, an emphasis on family and obedience to parents, a concern for the elderly and the poor, opposition to abortion, divorce and premarital sex, and the emphasis on the Protestant ethic of diligence, education and the attainment of skills (ibid.).

Through a detailed study of a group of software firms, Al James was able to identify how the above cultural traits influence corporate cultures, and how these corporate cultures in turn impact on the ability of Mormon firms to innovate and to grow. He discovered that series of tensions exist in this respect. Indeed, in terms of interfirm networking, Mormon companies would emphasise unity and mutuality, which translates into an enhanced ability to interact with other Mormon firms, but simultaneously limit their abilities to interact with (and hence learn from) non-Mormon firms (ibid., p.1205). In terms of exploitation of other firms' competences and outsourcing, Mormon firms' abilities are limited by their emphasis on self-sufficiency and autonomy (ibid., p.1206). Furthermore, instead of seeking venture capital for financing start-ups or expansion of their companies, Mormon managers prefer frugality, self-sufficiency and debt avoidance (ibid., pp.1206–7). Finally, instead of working long unsocial hours and having 'sleeping bags under the desk', Mormon firms prefer arrangements where working patterns do not compromise employees' commitments to their families and church. Equally, instead of afterwork socialising, Mormon firms are characterised by a 'rigid separation between work life and social life' (ibid., p.1209). Taken all together, there are Mormon cultural traits that in some cases promote, but in other cases severely constrain innovation potential of Mormon firms. This mixed picture can also be seen when one compares the performance of Mormon and non-Mormon firms in terms of revenue, R&D intensity and productivity (ibid., p.1211). One way or another, it is clear that firms' corporate cultures are shaped and conditioned by a strong regional culture in which they are embedded' (ibid., p.1212).

CONCLUSION

This chapter introduced a variety of concepts and theories that shed further light on economic geographies, or as Lee and Wills (1997) prefer to call it, 'geographies of economies'. Many (although not all) of these concepts have been influenced by evolutionary-institutional views. Collectively, they feed into a diverse group of insights that geographers call *new economic geography*. Implications of these insights for uneven development in the age of globalisation are not straightforward. Indeed, conflicting conclusions can often be drawn from these insights. One of these conflicting conclusions regards the very issue of uneven development. On the one hand, some authors would seem to suggest that achieving more balanced development in the new global knowledge economy will be easier. In part, this view is based on the assumption that factors influencing economic development are now less dependent on tangible resources then previously (e.g., raw materials during the Industrial Revolution) and that conditions for success (e.g., via supporting institutional arrangements) can be emulated even in the least developed regions and countries. On the other hand, economic geographers have pointed out that intangible sources of success in the knowledge economy are not easily transferred across space (geographical distance). In other words, key competitive strengths in terms of innovation, knowledge creation and overall 'learning' will continue to be concentrated in already established economic hot-spots. One way or another (and despite the fact that some basic concepts and assumptions remain to be debated) new economic geography offers some valuable insights on the economy and introduces new dimensions ignored by previous theories and concepts. Moreover, the 'cultural turn' in economic geography destabilises the conventional view of what is the economy. Ultimately, what will matter is whether these insights can be translated into practical policy (or political) actions that would help to create conditions for a more balanced, more equitable and more stable social and economic framework in the future. The policy challenges in the global era are enormous and the implications of economic geography insights for policy-making are going to be discussed in the final chapter.

FURTHER READING

On stages, cycles and waves theories, technical change and post-Fordism
Amin, A. (ed.) (1994) *Post-Fordism: A Reader*. (Oxford: Blackwell).
Coe, N.M., P.F. Kelly and H.W.C. Yeung (2007) *Economic Geography: A Contemporary Introduction*. (Oxford: Blackwell) Chapter 5.
Dicken, P. (2007) *Global Shift: Mapping the Changing Contours of the World Economy*. (London: Sage) Chapter 3.
Pike, A., A. Rodriguez-Pose and J. Tomaney (2006) *Local and Regional Development*. (London and New York: Routledge) Chapter 3.

On new economic geography approaches, including learning regions
Amin, A. and N. Thrift (1992) 'Neo-Marshallian Nodes in Global Networks', *International Journal of Urban and Regional Research* 16(4), pp.571–87.
Amin, A. and N. Thrift (eds) (1994) *Globalization, Institutions and Regional Development in Europe*. (Oxford: Oxford University Press).
Asheim, B. (1996) 'Industrial Districts as "Learning Regions": a Condition for Prosperity', *European Planning Studies* 4(4), pp.379–400.
Clark, G.L., M.P. Feldman and M.S. Gertler (eds) (2003) *The Oxford Handbook of Economic Geography*. (Oxford; New York: Oxford University Press).
Florida, R. (1995) 'Toward the Learning Region', *Futures* 27(5), pp.527–36.
MacKinnon, D. and A. Cumbers (2007) *An Introduction to Economic Geography: Globalization, Uneven Development and Place*. (Harlow: Pearson/Prentice Hall) Chapter 10.
Martin, R. (2002) 'Institutional Approaches in Economic Geography', in E. Sheppard and T.J. Barnes (eds) *A Companion to Economic Geography*. (Malden, MA: Blackwell), pp.77–94.

Morgan, K. (1997) 'The Learning Region: Institutions, Innovation and Regional Renewal', *Regional Studies* 31(5), pp.491–503.

Saxenian, A. (1996) *Regional Advantage: Culture and Competition in Silicon Valley and Route 128* (new edition). (Cambridge, MA and London: Harvard University Press).

Storper, M. (1995) 'The Resurgence of Regional Economies, Ten Years Later: the Region as a Nexus of Untraded Interdependencies', *European Urban and Regional Studies* 2(3), pp.191–221.

Storper, M. (1997). *The Regional World: Territorial Development in a Global Economy*. (New York and London: Guilford Press).

Critique of the new economic geography approaches

Hudson, R. (1999) 'The Learning Economy, the Learning Firm and the Learning Region: a Sympathetic Critique of the Limits to Learning', *European Urban and Regional Studies* 6(1), pp.59–72.

Lovering, J. (1999) 'Theory Led by Policy? The Inadequacies of the "New Regionalism" (illustrated from the case of Wales)', *International Journal of Urban and Regional Research* 23(2), pp.379–96.

MacKinnon, D., A. Cumbers and K. Chapman (2002) 'Learning, Innovation and Regional Development: A Critical Appraisal of Recent Debates', *Progress in Human Geography* 26(3) pp.293–311.

Martin, R. and P. Sunley (2001) 'Rethinking the "Economic" in Economic Geography: Broadening our Vision or Losing our Focus?', *Antipode* 33(2), pp.148–61.

Martin, R. and P. Sunley (2003) 'Deconstructing Clusters: Chaotic Concept or Policy Panacea?', *Journal of Economic Geography* 3(1), pp.5–35.

Sokol, M. (2004), 'The "Knowledge Economy": a Critical View', in P. Cooke and A. Piccaluga (eds) *Regional Economies as Knowledge Laboratories*. (Cheltenham, UK and Northampton, MA, US: Edward Elgar), pp.216–31.

On networks, trust and social capital

Amin, A. and N. Thrift (1992) 'Neo-Marshallian Nodes in Global Networks', *International Journal of Urban and Regional Research* 16(4), pp.571–87.

Amin, A. and N. Thrift (eds) (1995) *Globalization, Institutions and Regional Development in Europe*. (Oxford: Oxford University Press).

Martin, R. (2002) 'Institutional Approaches in Economic Geography', in E. Sheppard and T.J. Barnes (eds) *A Companion to Economic Geography*. (Malden, MA: Blackwell), pp.77–94.

On culture, ethnicity and gender

Coe, N.M., P.F. Kelly and H.W.C. Yeung (2007) *Economic Geography: A Contemporary Introduction*. (Oxford: Blackwell) Chapters 11, 12 and 13.

James, A. (2005) 'Demystifying the Role of Culture in Innovative Regional Economies', *Regional Studies* 39(9), pp.1197–216.

Lee, R. and J. Wills (eds) (1997) *Geographies of Economies*. (London: Arnold).

Saxenian, A. (1996). *Regional Advantage: Culture and Competition in Silicon Valley and Route 128* (new edition). (Cambridge, MA and London: Harvard University Press).

7. Economic geographies of the contemporary world

INTRODUCTION

As already pointed out in Chapter 2, powerful arguments have been made about the 'death of distance' and 'the end of geography' in this era of globalisation. Part of the argument is the claim that with the onset of information and communication technology (ICT) and other 'space-shrinking' technologies, geography does not matter at all, or that it matters less than hitherto. People, goods, services, money and information can apparently be moved freely across the globe, thus reducing the importance of geographical location and contributing to the equalisation and homogenisation of various localities, regions, countries and continents. This chapter will contrast such views with the ways in which globalisation works in the real world, by examining various aspects of economic globalisation and the ways they impact on people and places.

In doing so, the chapter will highlight the point that globalisation is best understood as a set of uneven processes (Dicken et al., 1997). In other words, (1) globalisation is a process or a set of processes (rather than an 'end state'); and (2) these processes unfold unevenly in time and space and have an uneven impact on different places (rather than equalising, homogenising and geography-eliminating effects). The development of ICT infrastructure is a case in point. As one of the sections in the chapter will show, ICT networks themselves are spread very unevenly in space and therefore they are probably reinforcing, rather than diminishing, inequalities between places. In addition to this, the chapter will challenge the assumption that globalisation is somehow 'natural', inevitable, irreversible and uncontrollable. Instead, the chapter will reinforce the view that the phenomenon of globalisation is socially created, regulated and governed by a myriad of institutions (see Coe et al., 2007, pp.51–2).

The chapter is organised around distinctive (although deeply interrelated) themes including: patterns of investment, production and trade; issues of global economic governance; trans-national and multi-national corporations; global cities; global finance; geographies of ICT and knowledge economies; geographies of emerging and transition economies;

and geographies of labour and migration. Equipped with the theoretical knowledge acquired in the previous chapters, you will be better able to appreciate how processes described within each of these themes are shaping economic geographies of globalisation.

GEOGRAPHIES OF ECONOMIC GLOBALISATION: INVESTMENT, PRODUCTION, TRADE AND CONSUMPTION

Economic globalisation has many dimensions, but one of the key features characterising the global economy is the growing economic interconnectedness of different parts of the world (Dicken, 2007; see also Box 1.1 in Chapter 1). This growing interconnectedness can be observed from the trends in investment, production and trade after the Second World War (WWII). While the globalising world economy did see major upturns and downturns, there nevertheless has been a long-term trend of increasing volumes of trade and investment across national borders in the last 50 years or so (a process again disrupted by the most recent global economic crisis). Cross-border investment in general, and *foreign direct investment* (FDI) in particular, saw a 'speculator acceleration' in the second half of the twentieth century (Dicken, 2007, p.37). Similarly, international trade has been growing significantly in that period. However, since the mid-1980s, the rate of growth of trade has been much outstripped by the rate of growth of FDI, suggesting that FDI has become 'the primary mechanism of interconnectedness within the global economy' (ibid., pp.37–8). One of the key drivers behind these trends is the operation of multi-national or trans-national corporations (MNCs or TNCs respectively), that is, large corporations operating across national boundaries and continents (see Dicken, 2007, pp.106–7 for a definition of a TNC).

Indeed, trans-national corporations, by their very nature, invest across national borders in order to create new production facilities or gain control over existing production facilities abroad. In doing so, they are shaping the patterns of production across the world (see more below). TNCs are also responsible for much of international trade. They account for about two-thirds of world exports of goods and services (ibid., p.38). Interestingly, a large share of this trade is in fact an intra-firm trade (i.e., movements of goods and services between different parts of the same firm). Perhaps as much as one-third of total world trade is generated by the intra-firm trade of TNCs (ibid.). As you can see from this, TNCs are major players in the global economy and therefore deserve closer examination (see the section on TNCs below). However, what is important to stress here is that TNCs have contributed in a major way to the re-shaping of the world's economic map.

Indeed, since WWII, a *new international division of labour* (NIDL) started to emerge (Fröbel et al., 1980), which involved a major shift in the distribution of agriculture, manufacturing and service activities across the world. Traditionally, the 'old' international division of labour has been characterised by a core-periphery structure that involved core (industrial) economies (most notably Britain, some Western European countries and later the US) and the agriculture-dominated periphery (the rest of the world). While the core economies were predominantly characterised by the production of manufactured goods, the periphery acted both as a marketplace for these manufactured goods and a source of raw materials and foodstuff for the core (see Dicken, 2007, pp.32–3). However, in the post-WWII period, manufacturing activities were increasingly relocated from the core economies to the periphery (Fröbel et al., 1980). This process accelerated in the period after the economic turbulence and oil crisis of the 1970s, contributing to a massive de-industrialisation of the core economies. The core economies, in turn, have progressively become dominated by the service sector (see also the stages theory in Chapter 6). At the same time, several economies in the periphery have experienced rapid industrialisation, most notably the 'Asian tiger' economies (such as Hong Kong, Korea, Singapore and Taiwan, and, later on Indonesia, Malaysia and Thailand) alongside the rising economic power of Japan (see also Dicken, 2007, p.43). In doing so, 'Asian tiger' economies have effectively become a semi-periphery and have become important consumer markets in their own right (Figure 7.1). However, since the 1990s, Japan has been stagnating and much of East Asia was shaken by an economic crisis in the end of the 1990s (see Krugman, 2008). Meanwhile, the growth in China and India has been accelerating (until the latest global economic crisis), in part as a consequence of their growing role in the new international division of labour through the expansion of their manufacturing sectors.

More recently, there has been a growing recognition that a *'newer' international division of labour* may be emerging (Coffey, 1996). Importantly, this 'newer' international division of labour may include the relocation of *service sector* activities from the core economies to semi-peripheral economies and beyond. An example of this is off-shoring of back-office service activities (such as call centres) to India (see Box 7.1). The shift can have cascading sectoral effects on semi-peripheral and peripheral economies (ibid.). With the collapse of state-socialism, the above processes have also involved the 'transition' economies of Central and Eastern Europe. Meanwhile, China and India have emerged as major players in the world economy (see also the section on emerging economies below).

Source: Photo by Martin Sokol.

Figure 7.1   'Asian tiger' economies: Bangkok, Thailand

While the above demonstrates the growing interconnectedness of the global economy, it is important to realise that the processes involved are highly uneven. Indeed, the global economic map that emerges from this is characterised by a strong concentration of economic activities (investment, production, trade and consumption) within the so-called 'global triad'. In a narrow sense 'global triad' refers to the core economies of the US, Western Europe and Japan, but it is now more commonly used to refer to the three macro-regions of North America, Europe and East Asia. These macro-regions play a leading role in the 'global' economy. For instance, much of the world's trade and FDI is in fact flowing within and between these three macro-regions at the expense of much of the rest of the world (Dicken, 2007, pp.38–62).

BOX 7.1 INDIA

India is the prime global destination for off-shoring back-office service activities, especially from English-speaking countries such as the US or UK. It is part of a wider process of relocating service activities to lower-cost locations, either directly (via directly owned subsidiaries) or through *outsourcing* (i.e., by subcontracting work to indigenous Indian firms or other third-party providers). This process accelerated in the 2000s, especially in the case of ICT-enabled services such as call centres (Figure 7.2), which are considered as being part of India's 'sunrise' industries. Thus, while

Source: Photo by Al James.

*Figure 7.2   Advertisement for call centre jobs via 'Dyn[a]mic
Placement' agency in north Delhi, India*

call centres and other back-office operations accounted for about 180,000 jobs in India in 2003, they increased sharply to over 700,000 jobs five years later and were expected to reach 1.4 million jobs in 2010. These jobs are mostly concentrated in established call centre hubs in Bangalore, Mumbai and Delhi, and emerging hubs of Pune, Kolkata, Chennai and Hyderabad. It is not difficult to imagine the forces behind this spectacular growth and to understand the reasons why multi-national corporations would want to relocate or outsource some of the service work to India. Clearly, one reason is that India has a large pool of well-educated and English-speaking people. The second, and crucial, reason is that this educated, English-speaking workforce is much cheaper to employ. Indeed, significant labour cost savings can be made here. This is very important for an industry where labour represents a major cost item (by far outweighing international telecommunication costs, which have fallen dramatically in recent years). Thus, while in the UK an average call centre worker would earn about £14,000 (US$20,000) annually, in India the same job can be done for about £1,400 or US$2,000 (i.e., for 10 per cent of the cost). From this point of view, the process of off-shoring can be seen as an example of companies moving their operations in search for cheaper labour (see Chapter 4).

What is interesting, however, is that £1,400 per annum is a respectable salary in India. It is three times the average national Indian income and twice the starting salary of a high school teacher, accountant, or entry-level marketing professional. It is no wonder then, that call centre jobs are very popular in India, especially among young, bright graduates. And in contrast to the UK, where call centre jobs are seen as 'dead end', for young Indians a call centre job is seen as the beginning of an international business career. However, despite the obvious attraction, call centre work is not easy. In the West, call centre employment is associated with a highly regimented labour process, long or unsociable working hours, increased workloads, less predictable work schedules, constant monitoring and so on. In India, call centre workers experience even greater workplace indignities and more challenging working conditions. This includes, for example, frequent night shifts (designed to serve Western customers in 'real' time), resulting in sleep deprivation, loss of appetite, digestive disorders and social isolation of call centre workers from friends and family. Also, it has been noted that call centre workers in India are subject to a form of 'cultural imperialism' by eroding traditional Indian identities (e.g., via adopting anglicised pseudonyms in communication with Western clients). Also, most call centre workers must undergo accent neutralisation to eradicate their 'mother tongue influence' to smooth customer interaction. Regardless, Indian call centre workers can be subject to verbal abuse, especially in cases when clients are unhappy about dealing with non-native speakers, or resentful of job losses in their home country resulting from the off-shoring process.

Off-shoring presents challenges in other ways as well. While clearly it has helped the Indian economy to gain momentum, much of it (including call centres) remains in the form of a subordinated role within an international division of labour. There are signs that this may change in the future and places like Bangalore, for example, are tipped to become future 'Silicon Valleys'. Meanwhile, despite all the progress made in terms of economic development, India remains not only one of the most populous countries in the world, but also the one with the highest number of people in poverty.

Source: Coe et al. (2007, pp.128–30); James and Vira (2009).

GOVERNING GLOBALISATION

Far too often, globalisation is described as a 'natural', inevitable, irreversible and uncontrollable force. It has been claimed that workers, firms, regions and whole countries have to adapt to it if they are to survive economically. However, as already mentioned in the introduction to this chapter, the process of globalisation is in fact socially created. Indeed, the process of globalisation is shaped, regulated and governed by a myriad of institutions (see Coe et al., 2007, pp.51–2). Local and regional authorities, national governments, international bodies, firms, labour organisations, non-governmental organisations (NGOs) and other institutions all shape economic globalisation one way or another. The key question is: what relative power do these various institutions have to influence the way in which economic processes work in the era of globalisation? Traditionally, nation-states (countries) have been responsible for the economic management of their national economies. However, as we have seen in the previous section, the global economy is characterised by the increasing interconnectedness between national economies. Consequently, the relevance of nation-states for economic management in the era of globalisation has been questioned. As we have already seen in Chapter 2 some argue that nation-states are simply irrelevant. This claim is often supported by the view that nation-states are going through the process of 'hollowing out' as key economic governance functions are being moved upwards (onto international and global institutions), downwards (onto local and regional bodies) and sideways (to private organisations). Others, on the other hand, maintain that nation-states still hold crucial economic functions.

The question about the (changing) role of nation-states in the process of globalisation is an important one. One way of dealing with it is to acknowledge that nation-states indeed still possess vital economic powers (ibid., Chapter 7) while recognising that their roles have been changing (Dicken et al., 1997). At the same time, it is important to recognise that new institutional arrangements have been emerging at various other geographical scales. Two key dimensions of this process ought to be highlighted here. First, there has been a marked tendency for nation-states to forge economic alliances with other nation-states at the macro-regional level (Coe et al., 2007, pp.211–13; Dicken, 2007, pp.187–204). This macro-regional integration may take various forms and is perhaps most advanced among the economies of the three macro-regions of the 'global triad' discussed in the previous section. In North America, the North American Free Trade Agreement (NAFTA) covers the US, Canada and Mexico. In Asia, the ASEAN Free Trade Area (AFTA) is in operation amid the growing economic integration in the East and South-East Asia. The European countries, meanwhile, have been pursuing their integration through the European Union (EU), 'by far the most highly developed and structurally complex of all the world's regional economic blocks' (Dicken, 2007, p.193). The EU is both a political and economic union and most of its members also share a single currency, the euro. One way or another, the EU, NAFTA, AFTA and other macro-regional groupings have a major impact on international trade and the way TNCs organise their production (see the next section).

The second set of institutional changes that has had a major impact on the governance of globalisation has taken place at the international/ global scale (Coe et al., 2007, pp.211–13). Indeed, a number of institutions have been created and specifically designed to promote economic cooperation at the global level. These institutions include the International Monetary Fund (IMF), the World Bank and the World Trade Organization (WTO). These institutions are sometimes referred to as the 'Bretton Woods trio' or Bretton Woods institutions, after the international conference held in Bretton Woods (New Hampshire, US) in 1944. The aim of the conference, attended by 44 nations, was to 'erect a new framework for the postwar global economy' (Ellwood, 2001, p.27). The IMF, the International Bank for Reconstruction and Development (IBRD; now widely known as the World Bank) and the General Agreement on Tariffs and Trade (GATT; the predecessor of today's WTO) emerged from the process. These institutions have played a significant role in governing economic globalisation ever since. The GATT and WTO, for instance, have been responsible for promoting international trade through the successive reduction of barriers (e.g., import tariffs) for trading goods. More recently, the reduction of barriers for trading in services has also been included on the agenda via the General Agreement on Trade in Services (GATS). The Bretton Woods institutions were also instrumental in promoting the mobility of capital, not least by urging countries to reduce barriers for FDI and other forms of investment across borders. Thus, collectively, the Bretton Woods institutions have major implications for the operation of national economies and international economic relations.

Having said this, it is important to stress that many of the policies pursued by these institutions have proved highly controversial. In particular, there is a concern that some policies are 'imbalanced and biased against developing countries' (e.g., see Ellwood, 2001, p.32). This echoes concerns about 'unequal exchange' between core and peripheral economies (which we discussed in Chapter 5) with the outcome of reinforcing, rather than reducing, global inequalities. As we have seen in Chapter 1, there is some evidence to suggest that this is indeed happening. This, in turn, raises the question of (a lack of) fairness in the way in which economic globalisation is being governed. The latest global financial and economic crisis has underlined the need to re-think global economic governance even further. We will return to this point in Chapter 8.

TRANS-NATIONAL AND MULTI-NATIONAL CORPORATIONS: GLOBAL COMMODITY CHAINS, PRODUCTION NETWORKS AND VALUE NETWORKS

The institutional landscape described above has, in turn, important implications for the operation of firms. Indeed, the progressive reduction of constraints on international trade and the movement of capital across borders have contributed to major shifts in the organisation of their

production. Major corporations with multiple production sites (traditionally confined to a national economic space) have been increasingly organising their production at the international scale. In other words, they have
become what is widely known as multi-national corporations (MNCs)
or, better still, trans-national corporations (TNCs). Driven by the profit
imperative, TNCs are seeking to exploit geographical differences in the
distribution and the cost of factors of production (e.g., natural resources,
capital and labour) and regulatory environments (e.g., taxes, trade barriers, state subsidies, etc.; Dicken, 2007, p.106). TNCs are thus characterised
by their ability and power 'to coordinate and control operations in more
than one country' (ibid.), even if they do not directly own all these operations (see below). Using the conceptual tools introduced in Chapter 5,
it could therefore be argued that TNCs are, either directly or indirectly,
contributing to the spatial divisions of labour, both within and between
national economies (see also the notion of the international division of
labour discussed above). TNCs, thus, can be seen as the primary 'movers
and shapers' of the global economy (and are often portrayed as a threat
to the economic autonomy of the nation-state; ibid.). In this context it is
important to note that the financial power of some major TNCs is now
comparable or larger than the financial power of some smaller nation-
states (see Ellwood, 2001, p.55).

Understanding the ways in which TNCs organise their economic
activities is therefore of crucial importance. Several approaches have been
devised to do that, including the *global commodity chain* (e.g., Gereffi,
1999), the *global production chain* (e.g., Henderson et al., 2002; Coe et al.,
2004) and the *value network* (Smith et al., 2002) approaches. While these
three approaches broadly point in the same direction, there are also important differences between them. Together they offer important insights into
the ways economic activities are being organised in the globalising world
(see suggestions for further reading at the end of this chapter).

GLOBAL CITIES, WORLD CITY NETWORK AND MEGA-CITY REGIONS

As we have seen in the previous section, production in the era of globalisation involves a complex web of economic activities and flows at various
spatial scales. Geographical expansion can be an important dimension of
the profit-seeking strategy of firms and corporations – for instance, in the
form of new, more profitable production sites, new markets, new points
of access to raw materials and so on (see also David Harvey's concept of
spatial fix discussed in Chapter 5). Trans-national corporations (TNCs),

in the search for profit, are thus constantly expanding the geographical scope of their operations (although in a very uneven way). However, while stretching their production network across the globe, TNCs are also faced with numerous challenges. Indeed, one of the major challenges is to coordinate these very complex and geographically dispersed production networks in a seamless way. The complexity and sophistication involved in managing and controlling the production, distribution and consumption processes is immense and growing. While in the past, large corporations used their in-house (headquarter) capacities to handle this, they are now increasingly relying on a vast array of specialised business service firms that provide a particular expertise in management consulting, IT consulting, marketing, advertising, logistics, finance, accounting and legal advice to mention but a few. Such business service firms are also referred to as advanced producer services (APS) or knowledge-intensive business services (KIBS).

However, while manufacturing activities now seem to be dispersed rather widely (although unevenly) across the globe (see also the concept of the new international division of labour discussed above), an interesting feature of business service firms or KIBS is that they tend to concentrate in the major cities of the core economies. Three cities of particular note are New York (Figure 7.3), London and Tokyo, which seem to act as the command and control centres of the global economy. This phenomenon has been examined by Saskia Sassen (2001) who described these cities as global cities. A key explanation that Sassen (2001, Preface, p.xx) offers for the spectacular concentration of service activity in global cities is that 'specialised service firms engaged in the most complex and globalised markets are subject to agglomeration economies' (a concept that we have discussed in Chapter 4). Sassen argues that:

> [t]he complexity of the services they need to produce, the uncertainty of the markets they are involved with either directly or through the headquarters for which they are producing the services, and the growing importance of speed in all these transactions, is a mix of conditions that constitutes a new agglomeration dynamic. The mix of firms, talents, and expertise from a broad range of specialised fields makes a certain type of urban environment function as an information centre. Being in a city becomes synonymous with being in an extremely intense and dense information loop. This is a type of information loop that as of now still cannot be replicated fully in electronic space, and has as one of its value-added features the fact of unforeseen and unplanned mixes of information, expertise and talent, which can produce a higher order of information. (Ibid.)

The 'new agglomeration dynamic' that Sassen describes thus ensures that complex, non-standardised, high-level service functions will concentrate in global cities. However, Sassen (2001) also noted that such a

Source: Photo by Martin Sokol.

Figure 7.3   Global cities: New York

concentration of advanced business functions goes hand in hand with growing social inequality in global cities. This is an important point and we will return to it in the section below on geographies of labour (see also Box 1.2 on London in Chapter 1).

Meanwhile, it is important to note that since specialised business service firms 'need to provide a global service' they need to engage with a 'global network of affiliates or some other form of partnership' (ibid., p.xxi). Indeed, there has been a growing recognition that advanced business services or KIBS themselves are 'globalising' (i.e., operating on a trans-national basis). In fact, some of them are becoming TNCs in their own right, with operations in major cities across the globe (see also the notion of the 'newer' international division of labour discussed earlier). Intra-firm and inter-firm linkages between KIBS of such cities are creating, what Peter Taylor and his colleagues call, the *world city network* (Beaverstock et al., 2000; Taylor, 2004). The world city network is formed by 'the myriad of flows between office towers in different metropolitan centres' (Taylor, 2004). The world city network analysis thus highlights the need to examine the nature of interconnections between cities, rather than the static attributes of individual cities (Coe et al., 2007, p.146; see also Chapter 4 for a discussion on the concept of connectivity).

More recently, economic geographers have also emphasised the need to examine information flows and interconnections within major cities or metropolitan centres. Traditionally, advanced business services have clustered in central business districts (CBDs). But more recently, various service functions have been decentralised away from city centres into secondary or tertiary locations in and around the edges of big cities and smaller urban centres in the hinterland. This creates a rather complex spatial division of labour and flows in and around major cities, which, in turn, can be better described as *city-regions*, or *mega-city regions* (Hall and Pain, 2006). The precise mechanisms of the emergence of such mega-city regions are still being studied, but one can imagine that the simultaneous processes of agglomeration and de-agglomeration are perhaps in operation at various spatial scales.

GLOBAL FINANCE

Globalisation of finance represents one of the most salient features of the contemporary world and its understanding is of critical importance for our societies and economies. One way to look at financial services is to see them as being part of the vast array of specialised business services (APS or KIBS) that assist major corporations in conducting their business (as we have discussed in the previous section). However, financial services are probably much more than that. Indeed, as one observer noted, the financial system has now achieved 'a degree of autonomy from real production unprecedented in capitalism's history' (Harvey, 1989, p.194). As such, the global financial system exercises a major influence on the way societies and economies work. A term, *financialisation*, is being used to describe this growing influence of financial capital over the economy and society. The importance of global finance in understanding the global economy cannot be overstated and deserves our foremost attention. However, the aim of this section is not to provide a comprehensive overview of global finance itself, but to highlight some ways in which global finance partakes in creating and re-creating uneven economic geographies.

Source: Photo by Martin Sokol.

Figure 7.4 Global finance: the City of London

Chapter 2 has presented the powerful argument put forward by Richard O'Brien about the 'end of geography'. His thesis is that the 'end of geography' with regard to international financial relationships is both inevitable and desirable. Inevitable, because as a consequence of the ICT revolution financial market regulators (nation-states) apparently no longer hold sway over their regulatory territory; and desirable, because both financial firms and their customers will benefit from the new locational freedom that globalisation of finance has to offer (O'Brien, 1992; cited in Martin, 1999a, p.15). However, the reality is much more complex and complicated. Indeed, there are a number of ways in which geography matters a great deal.

One can start by examining the claim that financial firms (thanks to space-shrinking technologies and the reduced constraints imposed by national regulators) will be free to locate virtually anywhere. However, the reality is that the global financial industry remains highly concentrated in a relatively small number of large financial centres. The three global cities, New York, London (Figure 7.4) and, to a lesser extent, Tokyo, dominate the map of global finance (see Coe et al., 2007, p.122; Dicken,

2007, pp.398–9). Clearly, strong (cumulative) agglomeration effects are in operation. This includes agglomeration effects in terms of:

- financial 'liquidity' (i.e., the size of the financial market in a given centre);
- technology (i.e., the presence of the most advanced information and communication technologies needed to support the operation of such a centre);
- the labour market (the presence of a large pool of highly skilled workers, which helps to attract further firms) (see Tickell, 2005, p.246).

In addition to this, there are less tangible factors in operation, perhaps of the kind alluded to by Sassen (2001; see above) and what in other contexts has been called *untraded interdependencies* (see Chapter 6). Together, these factors help to explain why the 'end of geography' is unlikely to apply to major financial centres.

Having said this, it is true that financial service firms are themselves 'globalising' (much like other APS or KIBS) and spreading their operations across the world. This process, however, is highly uneven and geographically very selective. Indeed, usually only specific (lower-order) financial functions are being decentralised, and usually to specific locations only. This process often takes advantage of favourable regulatory regimes such as very low taxes as is the case of some of the 'offshore' financial centres (e.g., see Dicken, 2007, pp.406–7). One way or another, the financial services industry is characterised by a refined and distinctive spatial division of labour. In other words, instead of spearheading the 'end of geography', the financial industry itself creates complex and uneven geographies (e.g., Sokol, 2007).

Finally, one needs to consider the effects that the operation of finance has on people and places around the world. While O'Brien boasts about the positive effects that globalisation of finance may bring to the 'consumers of financial services', the reality is, once again, much more complex. Billions of dollars' worth of assets and money are being traded through the global financial system every day, on a 24-hour basis. But who wins and who loses? One way of looking at global finance is through the prism of David Harvey's approach (discussed in Chapter 5). Financial capital and financial flows thus can be seen as an expression of accumulated surplus value, which is in a relentless need to search for further profitable opportunities in the circuits of capital around the world. Some of the capital flows into speculative financial instruments, helping to create a 'global casino'. Others end up as loans to developing countries, often reflecting and reinforcing the unequal relations of power between the rich creditors and poor debtors. Thus while some would argue that global flows of financial capital have beneficial effects for the global economy, others would point out that global finance also brings some global problems. Perhaps the two most important concerns involve the contribution of global finance to the increased instability of the global economy and the growing global inequality – the two issues already highlighted in Chapter 1. These two issues are of crucial importance and will be revisited in Chapter 8.

GEOGRAPHIES OF ICTs AND KNOWLEDGE ECONOMIES

While O'Brien's claims about the 'end of geography' specifically referred to financial services, much has been written about the ability of ICT to transform the overall economic fortunes of regions and whole nations (see Box 7.2). Many authors believe that with the emergence of the so-called post-industrial information society, or knowledge-based economy, the problems of uneven development created under industrial capitalism can be overcome. This expectation is based on the assumption that: (1) in the knowledge-based economy, information and knowledge replace tangible goods and materials as a dynamo for economic growth; and (2) information, knowledge and financial capital can be moved around the globe instantaneously without constraints, courtesy of ICT. Optimistic voices would therefore argue that even the most disadvantaged regions or nations (by their geographical location, poor transport infrastructure or pre-existing economic structure) have a fair chance to succeed in the global knowledge economy (see also Chapters 3 and 6). However, more cautious (and perhaps more realistic) approaches recognise that geographical location, alongside the pre-existing regional economic structures still matter and that tangible goods and physical movements continue to play an important role in contemporary economies. It appears that ICT-facilitated (virtual) movements do not replace physical movements and the associated need for transport, but often complement and sometimes even encourage such a need.

Further to this, it could be argued that despite their potential to overcome the friction of distance, ICT infrastructures themselves are very unevenly distributed in space. Prosperous metropolitan regions, economic hotspots and global cities (see above) are usually served first, attracting the most advanced telecommunications networks and services. Meanwhile, many geographically and economically peripheral areas that would benefit the most from the potential advantages of ICTs are often left behind. This

Source: Photo by Martin Sokol.

Figure 7.5   ICTs: global reach or 'digital divide'?

process of geographical differentiation is likely to accelerate further with
the continuing privatisation and liberalisation of telecommunications
and the retreat from the universal service provision previously imposed
by nation-states. Simply put, private telecom operators are likely to
cherry-pick the most profitable market segments (both geographically
and socially) while bypassing less profitable social groups, localities and
whole regions. In other words, ICT infrastructure is being overlaid on the
already very uneven social and spatial landscapes. The resulting 'digital
divide', therefore, can thus further reinforce previously existing uneven
development patterns (Figure 7.5). Such digital divides can be observed
at various spatial scales from local/urban (Graham and Marvin, 1996;
Graham, 1999) to regional, national and global (Wilson and Corey, 2000).

   However, what is important to recognise is that advances in transport
and telecommunications are also partaking in the emergence of new,
complex patterns of interregional and international divisions of labour
in both manufacturing and services, underpinned by global commodity
chains, expanding circuits of capital and value networks. Thus, instead
of the 'end of geography', we are perhaps witnessing a process of uneven
time–space compression, which is likely to produce new economic geographies with complex landscapes of winners and losers and differentiated
impacts on people and places around the world (Sokol, 2009).

BOX 7.2 IRELAND

Ireland, a small open economy in a geographical periphery of Europe provides an interesting example of spectacular economic change in a global context. Historically poor, agriculturally based and lagging behind its Western European counterparts, it was transformed in the 1990s into one of the wealthiest economies of Europe (Ó Gráda, 1997; O'Hogan, 2000; Clinch et al., 2002; Kirby, 2002). Not surprisingly, Ireland became a 'role model' (see Kirby, 2002, p.1) for other less-favoured countries and regions in the EU and beyond. Importantly, much of the growth experienced in Ireland has been driven by the capital city of Dublin. The regional economy of Dublin boasts high-tech manufacturing (ICT industry, pharmaceuticals/biometrics) and internationally traded services (e.g., financial services, software industry), thus contributing to Ireland's reputation as a 'thriving knowledge-driven economy' (IDA, 2003, p.6; see also Grimes, 2003; White and Grimes, 2004; Grimes and White, 2005). Dublin has been labelled as a 'new knowledge-based agglomeration' (O'Gorman and Kautonen, 2004), although the jury is still out as to whether it can be seen as a successful 'learning region' too.

Indeed, much of the success of Dublin can be attributed to wider structural advantages, national policy and EU subsidies, rather than to localised learning. The success of creating a 'knowledge-based agglomeration' in the software industry, for instance, can be attributed to low corporate taxes, generous employment grants and a readily available highly skilled but relatively low-cost work-force (ibid., p.468) facilitating the arrival of major foreign investors. The ICT infrastructure in Dublin also played a role. The availability of a sophisticated telecommunications system was a necessary (although not sufficient) condition for the creation of the International Financial Services Centre (IFSC), for instance, making Dublin a financial centre of European and international significance (Figure 7.6 and Sokol, 2007). It could be argued that through these developments, Ireland favourably re-positioned itself within the international division of labour.

The extent to which the use of ICTs and knowledge-based activities will transform the wider economy is unclear, however. As White and Grimes (2004, p.176) have rightly pointed out, '[t]rans-forming peripheral European regions into dynamic "learning

Source: Photo by Martin Sokol.

*Figure 7.6   US corporation Citi belongs to one of the biggest
employers in Dublin's International Financial Services
Centre (IFSC). The future of the IFSC will be tested by
the most recent global financial and economic crisis*

regions" remains a formidable challenge' and Dublin and Ireland are
no exception. Indeed, the very success of Dublin, for instance, is
undermining its own competitive position (e.g., in terms of labour
cost, housing cost and congestion) making future advances towards
a knowledge economy challenging indeed. Nevertheless, White and
Grimes (ibid., p.177) contend that a 'solid foundation for a knowledge-
driven economy has been constructed' in Ireland and Dublin.

More recently, the foundations for a continued economic prosperity have been shaken by the global economic crisis in 2008/09.
Ireland was previously the star economic performer in Europe,
hugely benefiting from globalisation. But having a small open
economy exposed to global forces meant that Ireland was also the
first EU member to go into recession. The economy contracted
sharply, the housing bubble burst and unemployment has been on
the rise. The government was forced to introduce emergency
measures (including pay cuts for public workers) to try to tame the
ballooning budget deficit amid fears that the EU or the IMF will step
in with even more draconian measures to bring the public finances
into balance. It remains to be seen what will be the long-term consequences of this crisis for the economic well-being of people in
Dublin and Ireland.

GEOGRAPHIES OF EMERGING AND TRANSITION ECONOMIES

Who wins and who loses in the global economy is of crucial importance
to the so-called emerging economies (sometimes also referred to as
emerging market economies or emerging markets). There is no precise
definition as to what constitutes an 'emerging' economy and there is
probably more than one way in which an economy can be labelled as
'emerging'. However, in business circles the term 'emerging market' has
a specific meaning and usually refers to an opportunity for investment
in more risky markets potentially earning higher rewards (as opposed
to established markets characterised by low risk and lower reward).
Examples of emerging economies/markets include large economies such
as Brazil, Russia, India and China (collectively known as 'BRIC'); and
also medium- and smaller-sized economies such as Argentina, Chile,
Indonesia, Malaysia and Thailand (plus transition economies such as the
Czech Republic, Poland or Hungary). Using the conceptual tools we have
discussed in Chapter 5, emerging economies or emerging markets can be
seen as emerging outlets for global financial capital (surplus value) to be
profitably invested (absorbed) into the new circuits of capital. In some
cases, the arrival of capital did indeed transform the fortunes of receiving
economies, such as those of India or China.

One way or another, the emergence of emerging economies forms part
of the process of economic globalisation. However, an important point to

note is that such a process is not 'neutral' as powerful interests are at play. Indeed, attempts to establish market economies around the world have been usually happening with a gentle nudge (or, as some would argue, with a less gentle push) from international organisations such as the IMF. The promotion of market solutions as a way of achieving prosperity has been at the top of their agenda, often with mixed results. Nowhere is this more visible than in 'transition' economies of Central and Eastern Europe and the former Soviet Union, to which we now turn.

Following the collapse of communism (state-socialism) at the end of the 1980s, nations of Central and Eastern Europe and the former Soviet Union have attempted to transform their economies from centrally-planned to liberal market economies. The progress towards the market and the degree of integration with the West has been carefully watched, monitored and supported by an array of international organisations (see, e.g. Smith, 2002).

The lessons learned in Central and Eastern Europe show that the process of transformation has been: (1) much more difficult than originally expected; and (2) very uneven in both social and spatial dimensions (see, e.g. Sokol, 2001). In part this reflects uneven ways in which 'transition' economies have integrated in the wider international division of labour and global production networks. Indeed, a complex map of winners and losers emerged in Central and Eastern Europe as a consequence (see also Chapter 1). Such a map of winners and losers also reflects the uneven ways in which regions and workers have been able to position themselves (or not) within value networks and flows (Box 7.3). The emergence of the marginalised households (Smith and Rochovská, 2006, 2007) and the 'working poor' in post-socialist cities (Smith et al., 2008) is a pertinent example of this process. This, in turn, raises questions about the position of labour within a global economy, which we will examine in the next sub-section.

GEOGRAPHIES OF LABOUR AND MIGRATION

The final section of this chapter is dedicated to labour. As already high-lighted in Chapters 3 and 5, it could be argued that all value comes from human labour. Workers are therefore central to the functioning of any economy. Without them, the global economy would come to a halt. However, despite the central role workers occupy in the global economy, often they do not reap the full benefits of their labour. Indeed, under capitalist social relations, labour is subject to exploitation and surplus value is appropriated by capitalists. Of course, times have changed since Marx

BOX 7.3 BRATISLAVA, SLOVAKIA

The region of Bratislava (Figure 7.7), capital of Slovakia, represents an interesting case through which opportunities and challenges of economic change in the emerging economies of Central and Eastern Europe can be explored. Indeed, the collapse of state-socialism in the late 1980s and the removal of the 'Iron Curtain' have opened up unforeseen opportunities for this small city-region (population 0.5 million); while at the same time creating a set of challenges. In the early 1990s Western observers tipped the Bratislava region, situated at the border with Austria, as the future 'Silicon Valley' of East-Central Europe (*Trend*, 1993; OECD, 1996, p.76). Factors such as labour cost, productivity, quality of life, research and development (R&D) level, proximity to Vienna (60 km or 40 miles) and strategic geographical position in the heart of the continent with easy access to markets were supposed to spur the creation of a dynamic and innovative region. Local experts, meanwhile, saw Bratislava as a key element 'for the creation and diffusion of innovation and successful passage of Slovakia to an information-oriented and knowledge-based society' (Ivanička, 1996, p.91).

A decade later, Bratislava emerged as one of the most prosperous regions in East-Central Europe (see Dunford and Smith, 2000; Eurostat, 2000). In part, this has been achieved through the high inflows of foreign direct investment (FDI) into both manufacturing (e.g., car industry) and services (e.g., banking and ICT-related services). However, 'Silicon Valley' dreams have not fully materialised (Sokol, 2003). Indeed, local innovation capacity remains limited and transformation to a 'learning region' hampered not least because of challenges and dilemmas associated with the simultaneous transformation to the market economy. For instance, local R&D capacity has been eroded during a painful economic transition and imposed national budgetary constraints. Also, the institutional landscape under transition has been characterised by turbulence in which the search for an '*animateur*' of regional development has proved to be rather challenging (ibid.). Combined with ongoing struggles over policy direction at the national level, still relatively weak institutional capacity at the regional level and the overall lack of financial resources, the environment for the creation of a 'learning region' is far from optimal. It remains to be seen whether the benefits stemming from the more recent EU (and eurozone) membership, improving institutional frameworks and policies to foster the knowledge-based economy at both national and regional levels, and growing cooperation with neighbouring Vienna will help to unlock the full potential of the Bratislava region.

It is important to note, however, that any success of the region of Bratislava needs to be seen in the context of a growing spatial divide within the country – between the dynamic regions in the west (including Bratislava) and increasingly marginalised Eastern Slovakia. Equally worrying is a growing social inequality. Within Bratislava itself, unemployment remains relatively low, but there are thousands of households struggling to survive on low incomes (Smith and Rochovská, 2006, 2007).

Source: Photo by Martin Sokol.

Figure 7.7   'Transition' economies: Bratislava, Slovakia

undertook his critical analysis of the capitalist society. However, certain crucial features remain. Importantly, massive social inequalities exist both between rich and poor people and also between rich and poor countries. While some would argue that globalisation has lifted millions of people out of poverty (e.g., Wolf, 2004), it is important to recognise that globalisation does not automatically bring benefits to everybody (see Chapter 1).

Indeed, the decades of globalisation have been associated with growing inequalities at various spatial scales (as explored in Chapter 1). Nowhere else are these inequalities more visible than in global cities. As Saskia Sassen (2001) noted, growing inequalities within global cities need to be seen in the context of global restructuring. Indeed, they are a reflection of a polarising employment structure with above-average earnings in the expanding advanced business services sector (KIBS), coupled with a growing army of low-paid, menial service jobs at the bottom of the employment ladder (see Box 1.2 on London in Chapter 1). Meanwhile, the 'middle' of the occupational structure has been disappearing in such cities as traditionally relatively well-paid manufacturing-related jobs have been relocated en masse to cheaper locations around the world.

Manufacturing that has been relocated or outsourced to less developed countries (LDCs), however, is not always unreservedly beneficial to local communities there. Indeed, there is growing evidence that workers at the frontlines of the global production networks (for instance, in the garment industries) have to endure precarious working conditions. In part, this reflects the way in which MNCs are organising their global commodity chains and often sub-contracting work to a large number of geographically dispersed factories. Sometimes, the factories in which these workers undertake the work are more akin to sweatshops (where low pay is combined with long working hours, job insecurity, minimum work protection and illegal work practices). Having said that, sweatshops can also be found in developed countries, often employing undocumented migrants, who form the most vulnerable group of workers. Advanced economies, regions and cities, continue to act as 'magnets' for labour (see also the concept of cumulative causation in Chapter 4), although clearly not everybody benefits from this (Figure 7.8).

Geographies of labour are therefore important, because they help us to better understand the roots of social inequalities and what can be done about these. In other words, geographies of labour see workers not only as passive victims of economic circumstances, but also as active agents who can shape economic processes to their advantage. In this context, the term *labour geographies* is perhaps more appropriate (Coe et al., 2007, p.269) as opposed to *geographies of labour*. However, while trying to reassert their power, workers have to contend with formidable forces, emanating from

Source: Photo by Martin Sokol.

*Figure 7.8   Migrant workers discussing their rights, Orange County,
California, US*

both the state and/or capital. One of the key challenges for the labour
movement arises from the fact that capital is (supposedly) increasingly
mobile, while labour remains relatively immobile. Thus, one of the tasks of
labour geographies is to explore, at various geographical scales, the differentiated power relations between labour, capital and the state. In doing so,
labour geographies can play an important role in helping us to understand
what economies are, how they work and how people make a living in such
economies. It is the well-being of people all around the world that should
be the ultimate aim and purpose of the global economy.

CONCLUSION

This chapter explored economic geographies of the contemporary world.
In doing so it engaged with the claim that globalisation leads to the 'death
of distance' or the 'end of geography'. The chapter supported the view that
globalisation itself is best understood as a set of uneven processes. Indeed,

globalisation processes unfold unevenly in time and space and have uneven impacts on different places (rather than equalising, homogenising and geography-eliminating effects). The development of ICT infrastructure is a case in point. As we have seen, ICT networks themselves are spread very unevenly in space and therefore they are probably reinforcing, rather than diminishing, inequalities between places. Various other aspects of the contemporary world have been examined in this chapter from the economic geography perspective, ranging from the patterns of investment, production and trade to issues of global economic governance, trans-national and multi-national corporations, global cities, global finance, emerging economies, labour and migration. Each and every one of these areas shows that 'the end of geography' is nowhere to be seen as the process creating the patterns of inequality and uneven development continues to operate in the contemporary globalising world. Further to this, and importantly, the chapter has challenged the assumption that globalisation is somehow 'natural', irreversible or uncontrollable, and its uneven impacts inevitable. Instead, the chapter supported the view that the phenomenon of globalisation is socially created, regulated and governed by a myriad of institutions. The globalisation process therefore can be managed for the benefit of people. This leads us to the consideration of policy options, which will be examined in the following chapter.

FURTHER READING

On geographies of economic globalisation (investment, production, trade, consumption)
Coe, N.M., P.F. Kelly and H.W.C. Yeung (2007) *Economic Geography: A Contemporary Introduction.* (Oxford: Blackwell).
Dicken, P. (2007) *Global Shift: Mapping the Changing Contours of the World Economy* (fifth edition). (London: Sage).
MacKinnon, D. and A. Cumbers (2007) *An Introduction to Economic Geography: Globalization, Uneven Development and Place.* (Harlow: Pearson/Prentice Hall).

On governing globalisation
Dicken, P. (2007) *Global Shift: Mapping the Changing Contours of the World Economy* (fifth edition). (London: Sage).
Ellwood, W. (2001) *The No-nonsense Guide to Globalization.* (London: Verso).
Stiglitz, J. (2002) *Globalization and its Discontents.* (London: Penguin).

On commodity chains, production networks and value networks
Coe, N.M., M. Hess, H.W.C. Yeung, P. Dicken and J. Henderson (2004) '"Globalizing" Regional Development: A Global Production Networks Perspective', *Transactions of the Institute of British Geographers* 29(4), pp.468–84.

Gereffi, G. (1999) 'International Trade and Industrial Upgrading in the Apparel Commodity Chain', *Journal of International Economics* 48(1), pp.37–70.

Henderson, J., P. Dicken, M. Hess, N. Coe and H.W.C. Yeung (2002) 'Global Production Networks and the Analysis of Economic Development', *Review of International Political Economy* 9(3), pp.436–64.

Smith, A., A. Rainnie, M. Dunford, J. Hardy, R. Hudson and D. Sadler (2002) 'Networks of Value, Commodities and Regions: Reworking Divisions of Labour in Macro-regional Economies', *Progress in Human Geography* 26(1), pp.41–63.

On global cities

Beaverstock, J.V., R.G. Smith and P.J. Taylor (2000) 'World City Network: A New Metageography?', *Annals of the Association of American Geographers* 90(1), pp.123–34.

Sassen, S. (2001) *The Global City: New York, London, Tokyo* (second edition). (Princeton and Oxford: Princeton University Press).

Taylor, P. (2004) *World City Network: A Global Urban Analysis*. (London and New York: Routledge).

Wills, J., K. Datta, Y. Evans, J. Herbert, J. May and C. McIlwaine (2009) *Global Cities at Work: New Migrant Divisions of Labour*. (London and New York: Pluto Press).

On geographies of global finance

Clark, G. (2005) 'Money Flows Like Mercury: The Geography of Global Finance', *Geografiska Annaler* 87B(2), pp.99–112.

Corbridge, S., N.J. Thrift and R. Martin (1994) *Money, Power and Space*. (Oxford: Blackwell).

Leyshon, A. and N.J. Thrift (1997) *Money/Space: Geographies of Monetary Transformation*. (London: Routledge).

Martin, R. (ed.) (1999) *Money and the Space Economy*. (Chichester: John Wiley).

On geographies of ICTs and knowledge economies

Castells, M. (1989) *The Informational City: Information Technology, Economic Restructuring and the Urban-regional Process*. (Oxford: Blackwell).

Castells, M. (2000) *The Information Age: Economy, Society and Culture, Vol. I: The Rise of the Network Society* (second edition). (Oxford: Blackwell).

Gillespie, A., R. Richardson and J. Cornford (2001) 'Regional Development and the New Economy', *European Investment Bank Papers* 6(1), pp.109–32.

Graham, S. (1999) 'Global Grids of Glass: On Global Cities, Telecommunications and Planetary Urban Networks', *Urban Studies* 36(5/6), pp.929–49.

Graham, S. and S. Marvin (1996) *Telecommunications and the City: Electronic Spaces, Urban Places*. (London: Routledge).

Wilson, M.I. and K.E. Corey (eds) (2000) *Information Tectonics: Space, Place and Technology in an Electronic Age*. (Chichester; New York: John Wiley and Sons).

On geographies of transition economies

Bradshaw, M. and A. Stenning (eds) (2004) *East Central Europe and the Former Soviet Union: The Post-Socialist States*. (London: Prentice Hall).

Pickles, J. and A. Smith (eds) (1998) *Theorising Transition: The Political Economy of Post-Communist Transformations*. (London: Routledge).

Smith, A. (2002) 'Imagining Geographies of the "New Europe": Geo-economic Power and the New European Architecture of Integration', *Political Geography* 21(5), pp.647–70.

Smith, A. and A. Rochovská (2007) 'Domesticating Neo-liberalism: Everyday Lives and the Geographies of Post-socialist Transformations', *Geoforum* 38(6), pp.1163–78.

Smith, A., A. Stenning, A. Rochovská and D. Swiatek (2008) 'The Emergence of a Working Poor: Labour Markets, Neoliberalisation and Diverse Economies in Post-socialist Cities', *Antipode* 40(2), pp.283–311.

Sokol, M. (2001) 'Central and Eastern Europe a Decade after the Fall of State-Socialism: Regional Dimensions of Transition Processes', *Regional Studies* 35(7), pp.645–55.

On geographies of labour and migration

Coe, N.M., P.F. Kelly and H.W.C. Yeung (2007) *Economic Geography: A Contemporary Introduction*. (Oxford: Blackwell) Chapter 9.

May, J., J. Wills, K. Datta, Y. Evans, J. Herbert and C. McIlwaine (2007) 'Keeping London Working: Global Cities, the British State and London's New Migrant Division of Labour', *Transactions of the Institute of British Geographers (New Series)* 32(2), pp.151–67.

Wills, J., K. Datta, Y. Evans, J. Herbert, J. May and C. McIlwaine (2009) *Global Cities at Work: New Migrant Divisions of Labour*. (London and New York: Pluto Press).

USEFUL WEBSITES*

http://www.globalvaluechains.org/ – website of the Global Value Chains Initiative hosted by Center on Globalization, Governance and Competitiveness at Duke University (US) – offers useful information for anyone interested in global commodity chains, global value chains and value networks.

http://www.lboro.ac.uk/gawc/index.html – website of the Globalization and World Cities Research Network (GaWC) maintained by the Geography Department at Loughborough University (UK). A very useful resource for anyone interested in cities and globalisation, with a large number of working papers and articles are available for free.

http://www.sed.manchester.ac.uk/geography/research/gpn/ – website on Global Production Networks hosted by the University of Manchester (UK) – offers research papers on topics on global production networks.

* All accessed 5 March 2011.

8. Economic geography and policy challenges

You must be the change you want to see in the world. (Gandhi)

INTRODUCTION

As we have seen in the previous chapter, the contemporary world is facing numerous economic and social challenges. Indeed, while economic globalisation is often claimed to bring benefits to those who participate in it, we need to recognise that the globalisation process itself is unfolding unevenly in both time and space. The impact of globalisation is therefore also uneven – with different outcomes for different people and places around the world. Some places and some people may benefit, while many others can find themselves on the losing side. As a consequence of this, inequality is growing at various spatial scales (see Chapter 1). Millions of people live and die in poverty. Uneven, unequal, unjust and unsustainable development represents a major challenge for contemporary societies. The devastating effects of the recent global financial and economic crisis made the imperative to search for alternative policy paradigms even more important and more urgent than ever before.

The aim of this chapter is to provide the reader with a basic introduction to existing policy paradigms before speculating on the policy options for the future. The chapter will discuss neo-liberal, Keynesian, state-socialist, 'Third Way' and alternative economic policy approaches, while highlighting the relevance of economic geography insights within each. The chapter will end up arguing that the most recent global economic crisis deserves a pause for thought and should stimulate thinking about policy frameworks that would contribute to a more balanced, equitable, just and sustainable development for the future. I will argue that economic geographers could contribute to this process by moving towards a 'newest' economic geography.

KEY POLICY PARADIGMS: NEO-LIBERALISM, KEYNESIANISM, SOCIALISM, 'THIRD WAY' AND ALTERNATIVE ECONOMIC APPROACHES

As we have seen in Chapter 1, the picture of inequalities in the contemporary world is rather complex. However, as we have seen, inequalities are substantial whichever way we measure them. Furthermore, in many cases, inequalities are rising at various geographical scales. As Roger Lee and David Smith put it: 'The reality is of an increasingly differentiated world, in the sense of unequal life chances at the local, national and global scales, and of growing fragmentation into sharply divided peoples and places' (Lee and Smith, 2004, p.4). Lee and Smith further argue that the role of scholarship is 'to identify and to create a better world' (ibid., p.11). Throughout this book we have been exploring many concepts and theories that help us to understand why economic geographies are so uneven. In this chapter, we turn our attention to the exploration of policy responses to the issues facing the contemporary world. As will become apparent, policy paradigms that will be introduced here are derived from different (and often diverging) theoretical standpoints (many of which we have explored earlier in this book). Consequently (and unsurprisingly), these approaches represent rather different (and often contrasting) views on the issue of inequality and how the issue should be tackled. Different policy approaches also have diverging views on the causes of the most recent global economic crisis and how it should be overcome (see Box 8.1).

Neo-liberalism

Neo-liberalism could be seen as the most pervasive policy paradigm of the last quarter of a century or so. It is based on the mainstream economic (neo-classical) view that the economy is a system characterised by a perfect competition between individual, profit-maximising economic agents, guided by the 'invisible hand' of the market. Therefore, it is based on the belief that the market is the best and the most efficient mechanism for allocating resources and factors of production, ensuring that the economy as a whole will reach equilibrium for the benefit of everybody (see Chapter 3). Problems such as unemployment are therefore perceived as temporary – the market will make sure that idle labour and idle capital will be matched. A similar principle applies to possible imbalances in the space-economy (see Chapter 4). Indeed, in neo-classical theory, regional disparities are only ever temporary since spatial inequalities set in motion the self-correcting movements in prices, wages, capital and labour to underpin the eventual convergence of economic and social conditions between regions (Martin and Sunley, 1998; cited in Pike et al., 2006, p.65). Likewise, technology diffuses over space, allowing regions to 'catch up'. Convergence in growth between regions occurs and spatial equilibrium is achieved (see Chapter 4).

Policies that are derived from these theoretical positions are very clear. If economies experience difficulties of achieving equilibrium (for example, unemployment is growing), this is because markets are not working efficiently. In other words, there are 'market imperfections' (e.g., too much government intervention). The policy efforts are thus directed to eliminate these market imperfections to allow market forces to operate in full force to restore equilibrium. A similar principle applies to the issue of uneven development. Spatial inequalities exist because the market is not working properly across space. Barriers to the mobility of capital and labour thus need to be eradicated and market forces need to be unleashed in order to let regional economies converge and achieve balanced development. However, empirical evidence supporting these views is weak (e.g. see Dunford and Smith, 2000; Pike et al., 2006, pp.66–7). In fact, as we have discussed in Chapter 4, there are good reasons to believe that even under perfect market conditions, regional divergence is more likely than convergence (see concepts of agglomeration, increasing returns and cumulative causation in Chapter 4). However, pro-market advocates do not see the market as a problem, but as a solution. If (regional) economies experience difficulties, this is because they are not exposed enough to market forces.

While Western economies have always relied on various forms of market liberalism, neo-liberal policies – based on free-market principles – have been reinvigorated in the 1980s with the emergence of right-wing, pro-market governments in the US and the UK (of Ronald Reagan and Margaret Thatcher respectively). The economic doctrine followed by the Reagan administration in the US is therefore sometimes also called 'Reaganomics'. De-regulation, privatisation, tight fiscal and monetary policies accompanied by a roll-back of the welfare state were among the features of such economic policies. In part, neo-liberalism emerged as a reversal, and a reaction to the perceived failure, of Keynesian economic policies (see below). Subsequently, a strong pro-market ideology took root within international organisations such as the IMF and the World Bank (Stiglitz, 2002, p.13). Policy prescriptions promoted by these organisations maintained the supremacy of market solutions to development problems and promoted neo-liberal globalisation (US style). Invariably, this involved drastic cuts in public spending and the overall reduction of the role of the state in the economy and an openness to international competition (by lifting barriers on trade and capital flows). In a way, this reflects a belief that capital mobility alone will bring about economic convergence between the richest and poorest nations. Aid for developing countries became conditional on such pro-market structural reforms (also known as structural adjustment programmes).

However, this one-size-fits-all 'medicine' prescribed by the IMF and the World Bank, left many 'patients' worse off. Indeed, IMF-sponsored policies led to 'disastrous consequences' (ibid., p.17) in many countries. Economic liberalisation left many developing countries further indebted to wealthy Western creditors, with debt repayments crippling their economies and their capacity to 'look after their citizens' (Ellwood, 2001, pp.46–52). In the few countries where pro-market solutions did work, the reforms usually benefited the better-off, with the poorest social groups hardest hit (Stiglitz, 2002, p.18). Furthermore, in many cases, economic gains achieved as a consequence of these harsh reforms have been wiped out in subsequent periods of economic turbulence. Thus, the neo-liberal policies of Bretton Woods institutions could be said to have contributed to growing inequalities within the global economy at various spatial scales, as we have explored in Chapter 1. Furthermore, it could be argued that, simultaneously, these policies contributed to the increased instability of the global economy. Indeed, within an increasingly interconnected global financial system and de-regulated financial capital flows, a crisis occurring in one place can spread easily throughout the system, with pain being felt across the world. The IMF proved to be ill-equipped to safeguard global economic stability, the reason for which it was originally set up. In fact, its critics have pointed out that it was the very IMF actions that aggravated the problem, as was the case in the Asian financial crisis in the late 1990s (Ellwood, 2001; Stiglitz, 2002). The most recent example has involved the 'global credit crunch', which has escalated into a full-blown global financial crisis (see Box 8.1). Therefore, while neo-liberalism remains a dominant policy paradigm, its merits are increasingly questioned and the need to explore alternative policy frameworks grows.

Keynesianism

Keynesianism is one such alternative policy paradigm. In contrast to neo-liberalism, Keynesianism is based on the recognition that markets are not necessarily self-regulating. Far from it! Capitalist market economies are prone to periodic economic crises and rising unemployment during such crises makes things worse. Given that the market is unable to cope with this, there is a need for the state to intervene to bring back equilibrium and to achieve full employment. Therefore, in contrast to neo-liberalist views,

Keynesianism sees government intervention not as part of the problem but as part of the solution.

The foundations of Keynesian economics were laid down by a British economist John Maynard Keynes back in the 1930s. It was an era of deep economic crisis and high unemployment across the capitalist world. Ellwood summarises Keynes's arguments as follows:

> the free market, left on its own, actually creates unemployment. Profitability . . . depends on suppressing wages and cutting costs by replacing labour with technology. In other words, profits and a certain amount of unemployment go hand-in-hand. So far so good, at least for those making the profits. But then Keynes showed that lowering wages and laying off workers would inevitably result in fewer people who could afford to buy the goods that factories were producing. As demand fell, so would sales, and factory owners would be forced to lay off even more workers. This, reasoned Keynes, was the start of a downward spiral with terrible human consequences. (Ellwood, 2001, p.26)

In other words, Keynes argued that it was the lack of sufficient *aggregate demand* in the economy that explains economic downturns, and that government policies could help to stimulate demand (Stiglitz, 2002, p.11), via public spending.

The above explanation of the causes of economic crises is remarkably similar to the Marxist analysis we have explored in Chapter 3. Indeed, it could be argued that 'John Maynard Keynes, the father of state economic management and much of modern macroeconomics, owed a debt to Marx for some key insights into the dynamics of the capitalist system' (Dicken and Lloyd, 1990, p.357). Unlike Marx, however, Keynes did not advocate the end of capitalism. Indeed, Keynes's objective was not to abolish capitalism, but to make it run more smoothly and perhaps more equitably. For these reasons, Keynesian policies have been mostly favoured by social-democratic governments. In Sweden and other Scandinavian countries, for instance, Keynes-inspired policies have been accompanied by large public expenditure (e.g., on education and health care), generous welfare provision and progressive taxation systems that support the redistribution of income from the well-off towards the less well-off. No doubt this contributed to a more stable economic growth combined with a more equitable spread of wealth within a society. (As we have noted in Chapter 1, Scandinavian countries have the lowest Gini coefficient among advanced capitalist countries.)

Keynesian ideas have also played an influential role in conceptualising uneven development. The concept of cumulative causation that we have explored in Chapter 4 is a case in point (see also Pike et al., 2006, pp.69–77). Drawing on these insights, Keynesian approaches to regional policies involve an attempt to reverse *backwash* effects by redistributing resources and stimulating demand in weaker regions (e.g., see the growth pole strategy described in Pike et al., 2006, pp.75–6). Again, as we can see, the role of government is central in ensuring more balanced development, rather than leaving it to market forces.

Keynesian ideas also played an influential role at the international level. Keynes himself was one of the key delegates at the Bretton Woods conference. His influence at the conference was 'significant' although 'he did not win the day on every issue' as powerful US interests prevailed on a number of fronts (Ellwood, 2001, p.27). Nevertheless, Bretton Woods institutions were originally conceived as a way of regulating the global economy and preventing global economic crises. Keynesian policies proved very popular among many national governments after WWII and this coincided with the period of sustained growth during a so-called post-war 'golden era'. However, by the end of the 1960s, the limits of the system had started to show. The economic crisis of the 1970s (combined with the 'oil crisis') was perceived as a failure of Keynesianism. Keynesian consensus started to unravel, giving way to more pro-market, neo-liberal policies, as discussed above. As we have seen earlier, the Bretton Woods institutions have also changed. The IMF is a case in point. While it was founded on 'the belief that markets often worked badly, it now champions market supremacy with ideological fervour' (Stiglitz, 2002, p.12). John Maynard Keynes 'would be rolling over in his grave were he to see what has happened to his child' (ibid., p.13). More recently, Keynesian ideas have been surfacing again, hand-in-hand with the perceived shortcomings of the neo-liberal development model (see Box 8.1).

State-socialism

The idea of socialism is mostly derived from the writings of Marx. As we have seen in Chapters 3 and 5, Marx believed that due to its internal contradictions, capitalism will eventually collapse, giving way to a new society. Having said that, Marx provided very little detail on how such a new society would actually work, except by arguing that socialism would be a transition phase on the way to communism, following the collapse of capitalism. Thus, unlike Keynesianism, which aims to make the capitalist system more stable, the idea of socialism involves the demise of capitalism altogether. Under socialism, capitalist social relations are to be replaced with a new set of social relations, free from exploitation. In order to achieve this, private ownership of the means of production would need to be abolished and workers would regain control over the production process. Marx predicted that the socialist revolution would happen in the most advanced capitalist countries (i.e., where the contradictions would be the sharpest).

However, as we know, the course of history has been different. A successful socialist revolution took place in 1917 in Russia, an emerging industrial power, but not the most advanced capitalist country by any measure. The newly established Union of Soviet Socialist Republics (USSR or the Soviet Union for short) has, in addition, faced numerous challenges including the carnage of WWII. The construction of a socialist society thus happened in historical circumstances very different from those expected by Marx. However, after WWII, the communists took control of much of East-Central Europe and won power in China and other Asian countries (Vietnam, Laos, North Korea). Several other countries in Africa and Latin America were also leaning towards socialism. In other words, the group of countries that attempted to implement socialist ideas was very diverse. Consequently, and contrary to a popular perception of the existence of some sort of monolithic communist system, policies pursued by individual 'communist' countries were often very different. The extent to which these countries achieved socialism is an open question.

The system that was in place in East-Central Europe (e.g., in Czecho-Slovakia), for instance, can be at best described as 'state-socialist' (Smith, 1998). Features of such a system included the eradication of private property through nationalisation of existing industries, collectivisation of agriculture and state involvement in all spheres of economic, social, cultural and political life. In theory, all power was supposed to be held by workers, but in practice, the Communist Party was in charge. An important point is that the market was basically suspended and replaced by the 'central planning system' as a mechanism for the allocation of resources. State-socialist economies are known for their 'inefficiency'. However, it should be noted that economic and social programmes run by the communists did translate into real improvements of living standards for millions of people. Also, state-socialist countries made some progress in eradicating social inequalities and achieving more balanced development, although sometimes by creating unsustainable economic structures (ibid.).

The limits to the state-socialist development model started to show in the 1970s, resulting in an eventual collapse in the 1980s. The reasons for the collapse are still not well understood. However, most people believe (rightly or wrongly) that the lack of market forces and the failure of the central planning system to manage the economy are to be blamed. Consequently, state-socialist countries embarked on a painful 'transition' from centrally-planned to market-driven economic models (see, e.g. Sokol, 2001). The introduction of free-market capitalism in the 1990s thus

Source: Photo by Martin Sokol.

*Figure 8.1   Bratislava, Slovakia: formerly state-owned shopping centre
Prior, now owned by global retail chain Tesco*

represented a complete reversal of social and economic processes (Figures
8.1 and 8.2). Rapid economic liberalisation, privatisation, de-regulation
and the overall withdrawal of the state from economic affairs were among
the policies pursued, often with the support of international organisations
such as the IMF (see above). However, as we have already seen in Chapter
1, economic transformation has been more difficult than predicted. Stiglitz
(2002, p.6) has noted, for instance, that instead of 'unprecedented prosperity', the introduction of a market economy has brought 'unprecedented
poverty'. He argues, that 'in many respects, for most of the people, the
market economy proved even worse than their Communist leaders had
predicted' (ibid.). Indeed, even if some countries have achieved 'progress',
this has often been at the expense of rising social and spatial inequalities
(see also Box 7.3 in Chapter 7). In addition to this, many post-socialist
countries were among the hardest hit in the most recent global economic
crisis (see Chapter 1). To a large extent, the difficulties experienced by
many former state-socialist economies of East-Central Europe and the
former Soviet Union, contrast with a dynamic growth of China, which

Source: Photo by Martin Sokol.

*Figure 8.2   Laos, one of the few remaining communist states, has recently
               started opening up its economy*

has chosen a more gradual approach in introducing market systems and in
integrating with the world economy (e.g., see Stiglitz, 2002).

The 'Third Way'

The 'Third Way' emerged from the intellectual vibrations of the alternative (heterodox, evolutionary) economic approaches, in particular those
emphasising the emergence of the knowledge-based economy (see Chapters
3 and 6). As a political project and policy paradigm, the 'Third Way' could
be seen as an attempt by social-democratic political parties in the West to
define a way forward, after other 'ways' have failed. As Anthony Giddens,
one of the key proponents of the 'Third Way' has argued, '[f]ollowing the
decline or collapse of the other "ways", third way politics has to look for a
different basis of social order' (Giddens, 2000, p.55). It is clear that the collapse of state-socialism (described above) played a major role in the formu-
lation of the 'Third Way'. Indeed, as Giddens (ibid., p.28) has argued, after
the collapse of state-socialism in 1989 'we can't think of left and right in the
same way as many once did'. Further to this, the 'Third Way' recognises

other major changes in the world. In particular, it aims to 'respond to the great social transformations of the end of the twentieth century: globalization, the rise of the new knowledge-based economy, changes in everyday life, and the emergence of an active, reflexive citizenry' (ibid., p.65). Obviously, Giddens has argued, 'social democrats should not join with the free-marketeers in denigrating the state and all its works' (ibid., p.57). However, the 'Third Way' is distinctly different from the old Keynesian social-democratic approach. Indeed, in major contrast to Keynesianism, which favoured *demand-side* intervention (e.g., via public spending on major public works), 'Third Way' economics focuses instead on the *supply side* (e.g., spending on education, which will produce 'knowledge workers' for the 'knowledge-based economy'). In terms of regional policies, the 'Third Way' solutions favour supply-side interventions (supporting learning, knowledge creation, innovation, social capital, etc.), rather than providing heavy subsidies for industries in less favoured regions.

'Third Way' proponents are well aware that the rise of the 'knowledge economy' has been accompanied by increasing social and spatial inequalities (Leadbeater, 2000, pp.11–12). Nevertheless, it is believed that these inequalities should be addressed by 'organising our lives and our societies around self-improvement and learning' (ibid., p.223). Furthermore, people and nations should open themselves to globalisation, because '[i]f we turn our backs on the global economy, we turn our backs on the most vital force in modern societies: the accelerating spread of knowledge and ideas' (ibid., p.xi). Indeed, it is '[t]hrough global trade in products and services people learn and exchange the ideas that in turn drive economic growth' (ibid.).

Alternative Approaches

While the above 'Third Way' vision looks impressive, critics would argue that it is but an ideological smokescreen for a de facto embracement of the neo-liberal agenda. In other words, capitalism has not been superseded by the supposed arrival of the 'knowledge economy' and the 'Third Way' fails to address some key issues stemming from capitalist social relations (which remain pervasive). In the search for 'real' alternatives, some people are turning their attention towards non-capitalist economic models. Examples of such alternatives include 'community economies' promoted by Gibson-Graham (2006), local exchange trading systems (LETS) described by Lee (1996) or worker-controlled cooperatives such as Mandragon Cooperative (see Coe et al., 2007, p.279, Box 9.5; Dicken, 2007, pp.550–51). The crucial question, however, is whether such alternatives have a potential to be implemented on a global scale.

BOX 8.1   WALL STREET AND THE GLOBAL FINANCIAL AND ECONOMIC CRISIS

If finance, in the words of Martin Wolf (2010, p.1), is 'the brain of the market economy', then Wall Street is the key part of that brain. Situated in Manhattan, New York City, it is not only the biggest financial centre in the US, but also (alongside London) the biggest and most important financial centre in the world. There is little doubt that Wall Street has been one of the biggest engines behind the process of economic globalisation. Unfortunately, Wall Street was also in the epicentre of the global financial and economic crisis that shook the world towards the end of the first decade of the twenty-first century, when not only the 'brain' suffered a massive stroke, but the entire global market economy itself was on the brink of collapse.

As the crisis started to unfold in 2007 and grew in intensity and scale, so the blame game erupted, looking for those responsible. The list of suspected culprits is long. At the beginning, when the sub-prime mortgage market in the US imploded, the press quickly pointed a blame finger at irresponsible borrowers – those apparently careless individuals and families on low incomes that bought their homes using mortgages that they were unable to repay. They borrowed huge amounts of money, it was claimed, and lived beyond their means, relying as they were on the expectation that the property prices will always go up. In some people's eyes, home repossession is a logical punishment for such fecklessness, once the financial overstretch hits the limits. However, as soon as the crisis started to bite well beyond the sub-prime sector and the increasing rate of repossessions was bringing the entire US housing market down, the list of the suspected perpetrators started to expand. The attention shifted from borrowers to lenders. Banks and mortgage companies were blamed for luring unsuspecting customers into mortgage products and in doing so enticing them into massive debts that they knew they could not pay back. Sure enough, repayments became unsustainable, once introductory teaser-rates expired and interest rates went up.

However, rather than this being an isolated incident of a bad behaviour among some mortgage lenders engaging in 'predatory lending' practices, it soon became clear that mortgages in general, and sub-prime mortgages in particular, were very much at the heart of the operation of the entire financial system. Indeed, it became apparent that mortgage products represented a major source of business for Wall Street firms and global investment banks. Mortgages of thousands of people were repackaged and sold on international financial markets in a form of mortgage-backed securities (MBS) by major Wall Street financial players, while making hefty profits. The failure of derivatives such as MBS was at the heart of the crisis. Ironically, they were designed to reduce the risk to investors buying these products. Indeed, MBS were sold as safe investments – often with AAA-rated 'seal of approval' by major credit rating agencies. Thus, as soon as these safe investments turned out to be 'toxic assets' with doubtful value, the anger turned on the credit rating agencies as well. Questions were being asked how this was allowed to happen. As it turned out, far from being independent and impartial, credit rating agencies directly benefited from the process of such credit rating. All this (and much more) shook the confidence in the entire financial system and the way Wall Street works.

But as the crisis gathered pace, questions also started to be asked about the role of government (and regulators) in creating this mess. Regulators were accused of 'being asleep behind the wheel'. The US Federal Reserve (and central banks elsewhere) was accused of keeping interest rates too low for too long, thus fuelling the borrowing bonanza. And so it went on. From feckless borrowers, to greedy Wall Street bankers, to short-sighted regulators, it seemed that just about everybody was to be blamed for this economic catastrophe.

In parallel to this, there has been a growing debate in academic circles about this economic calamity and various terms have been used to describe it. Reinhart and Rogoff (2009, p.xiv) refer to it, rather euphemistically, as 'the Second Great Contraction' (the first one being the Great Depression of 1930s). Meanwhile, Foster and Magdoff (2009, p.11) call it 'the Great Financial Crisis' and Joseph Stiglitz (2010, p.xi) uses the term 'the Great Recession'. Regardless of labelling, there is very little doubt that the crisis that begun in 2007 was 'the most destructive economic event of the last eighty years' (Davies, 2010, p.2). However, despite the consensus about the scale of the crisis, there is very little agreement among economists about the underlying causes of it. Howard Davies (2010) himself presented the list of no less than 38 potential causes, some more serious than others, from derivatives ('financial weapons of mass destruction') to hormones (in particular, testosterone, which apparently causes irrational risk-taking by male traders). Crucially, the lack of consensus on the causes of the crisis also means that there are huge disagreements about how it should be tackled. Among the plethora of approaches, however, three contrasting positions on the crisis can be identified:

- Mainstream (neo-liberal) economic perspective/market fundamentalism;
- Keynesian perspective;
- Marxist perspective.

Mainstream (neo-liberal) economic perspective maintains that markets work fine and should be allowed to operate unconstrained. This kind of 'market fundamentalism' promotes the idea that markets are efficient and self-correcting. Crises happen for a reason – they are means through which markets allow for a 'market correction' to happen, before equilibrium can be restored in the economy. Government should not intervene. Any intervention by the government distorts the markets. Any attempt to rescue a failing company creates a 'moral hazard' – a signal to market participants that if they do get into trouble, they will always be rescued by the government. Market fundamentalists argue that this will only support irresponsible behaviour of market participants and therefore the government should not bailout any casualties of the crisis. Reasoning like this was perhaps behind the decision not to save Lehman Brothers from collapsing in September 2008. But instead of reassuring markets, the collapse of Lehman Brothers sent shockwaves through the global financial system. If one of the oldest and biggest investment banks in the world can collapse, no one is safe. Policy-makers were painfully reminded that some financial institutions have grown so big that they are now too big (and too interconnected) to be allowed to fail. Subsequently, the government intervention proved crucial in saving the entire system from collapsing. Despite all this, 'market fundamentalism' remains rather dominant in policy-making circles, especially on the right of the political spectrum. Their view is that the governments have to *reduce* their intervention in the economy and impose austerity measures to cut their way out of the crisis.

Another frequently aired mainstream economic view is that the cause of the crisis lies with the 'imbalances' within the global economy (e.g., see Wolf, 2010). According to this account the crisis is an expression of imbalance in economic relations between the US and China, where the Chinese are producing, exporting and saving too much, while the Americans are importing, consuming and borrowing too much. The balance can be restored if only the Chinese started to consume more of their own products and thus helped to spend some of the 'global savings glut'. While the merits of this point are shared beyond the neo-liberal camp (see below), for market fundamentalists the debate about the global imbalances conveniently shift the attention away from the failings of the US economy, while maintaining the neo-liberal mantra of market superiority and its ability to deliver equilibrium.

In contrast to market fundamentalism, the starting position of the *Keynesian approach* is that, in the light of the current crisis, 'only the deluded . . . would argue that markets are self-correcting and that society can rely on the self-interested behaviour of market participants to ensure that everybody works honestly and properly – let alone works in a way that benefits all' (Stiglitz, 2010, p.219). Indeed, Keynesian economists would argue that 'markets do not work well on their own' and that '[g]overnment needs to play a role' (ibid., p.xii; see also Krugman, 2008). Indeed, the crisis proved that market fundamentalists are wrong in assuming that 'unfettered markets by themselves can ensure economic prosperity and growth' (ibid., p.xiii). In contrast to market fundamentalists' view that the crisis is just an 'accident' in the otherwise successful system (and 'no one would suggest that we stop driving cars just because of an occasional collision'; ibid.), Keynesians would argue that 'the problems are systemic' (ibid., p.xix) and that the crisis uncovered 'fundamental flaws in the capitalist system' (ibid., p.xxi). In particular, Stiglitz has an issue with 'the peculiar version of capitalism that emerged in the latter part of the twentieth century in the United States', that is, the 'American-style capitalism' (ibid.). To put it differently, neo-liberalism itself is a part of the problem. Stiglitz, however, points out that it has been hard to see the flaws of the American-style capitalism, not least 'because we Americans wanted so much to believe in our economic system. "Our team" had done so much better than our arch enemy, the

Soviet block' (ibid.). Yet, as it turns out, the US economy needs much more than just 'fixing a few minor problems or tweaking a few policies' (ibid.).

Stiglitz would agree with mainstream economists that the global imbalances are partly to blame. Indeed, he points out that the American recovery needs strong global economy, and that 'it may be difficult to have a strong global economy so long as part of the world [e.g., China] continues to produce far more than it consumes, and another part [US] . . . continues to consume far more than it produces' (ibid., p.xxiii). However, Stiglitz makes it clear that the causes of the problem are at home, not least in the form of 'a pile of debt that supported unsustainable levels of consumption'. The debt, in turn, can be linked to another 'deeper problem', namely that the US is 'a society where even those in the middle have seen incomes stagnate for a decade, a society marked by increasing inequality' (ibid., p.xxii). For Keynesians, the crisis is precisely the moment when the government needs to intervene *more*, not less. In other words, the government should support the economy via increased spending, even if this means increasing deficit (e.g., see ibid., p.59), and in a way that will support a fairer distribution of income in the society. Stiglitz himself argued for a substantial stimulus package that would 'stimulate the economy in the short run and strengthen the country for the future' (ibid., p.58).

In the long run the aim of the Keynesian approach would be to 'restore our sense of balance between the market and the state, between individualism and the community, between man and nature, between means and ends' (ibid., p.296). As Stiglitz argues:

[w]e now have the opportunity to create a new financial system that will do what human beings need a financial system to do; to create a new economic system that will create meaningful jobs, decent work for all those who want it, one in which the divide between the haves and have-nots is narrowing, rather than widening; and, most importantly of all, to create a new society in which each individual is able to fulfil his [or her] aspirations and live up to his [her] potential, in which we have created citizens who live up to shared ideals and values, in which we have created a community that treats our planet with the respect that in the long run it will surely demand. (Ibid., pp.296–7)

The *Marxist approach* bears some resemblance to Keynesian analysis in that the inequalities are considered among the root causes of the crisis. In this sense, Marxists re-affirm their conviction that the inequality is directly interrelated to the instability of the capitalist economy (see also Chapters 3 and 5). Indeed, for a capitalist economy to function, someone has to consume what is being produced. But, as Foster and Magdoff (2009, p.27) remind us, how much is spent on consumption goods depends on the income of the working class (while the overwhelming proportion of the income of capitalists is devoted to investment). Increasing inequality under capitalism creates its 'age-old conundrum': 'an accumulation process (savings-and-investment) that depends on keeping wages down while ultimately relying on wage-based consumption to support economic growth and investment' (ibid.). The only way 'to square the circle' is for working people to borrow. In other words, economic growth is underpinned by growing consumer debt, chiefly via credit cards or refinanced mortgages (ibid., pp.28–36). This can work for some time. But, as Marxists would argue, this does not solve the problem, it only pushes it further into the future (see also Harvey, 2010). Sooner or later, the crisis will emerge. Foster and Magdoff (2009) suggest that finance has been underpinning the US economy for some time now. They argue that from being 'a modest helper to the capital accumulation process', the financial sector gradually became a 'driving force' (ibid., p.18). Speculative finance, in their words, 'became a kind of secondary engine of growth', while the primary engine (investment in productive capacity) remained weak, since at least the 1970s (ibid.). This corresponds to 'a shift of gravity of the economy from production to finance', also known as 'financialisation' (ibid.). The problem is, according to Foster and Magdoff (ibid., p.21), that 'the financialisation process itself is now in crisis'. Consequently, they argue, '[t]he most likely prospect therefore is a prolonged, deep stagnation' (ibid.).

For Foster and Magdoff (2009) this requires a dramatic solution that differs sharply from the Keynesian one. Indeed, while Keynesians would argue for a new, better form of capitalism (see above), Marxists maintain that the solution must be found beyond capitalism. Foster and Magdoff (ibid., p.139) thus argue that 'in contradiction of Keynes's dream of a more rational capitalism' the problems cannot be resolved 'without moving beyond the system itself'. Foster and Magdoff (2009) conclude that 'the entire political-economic structure should be replaced, brick by brick' (p.23) with a 'real political and economic democracy' – socialism (p.140).

There are many other views on what caused the crisis (e.g., see Schwartz, 2009, for a sophisticated account) and what should, or should not, be done (e.g., Williams and Elliot, 2010). The future will tell which way it will go. However, in 2010, there was a growing feeling that we have witnessed a 'terrible waste of a good crisis' (French and Leyshon, 2010) and that 'hyper-neoliberalisation' (ibid., p.2550) was winning the day. If so, then this may also mean that some of the underlying problems will not be resolved. In fact, it may be expected that such hyper-neoliberalisation will be accompanied by growing social and spatial inequalities. As a con-sequence, further financial and economic turbulence can be expected in future, perhaps with even greater social, economic, political and environmental consequences than seen so far.

POLICY OPTIONS FOR THE FUTURE

The previous section provided some basic knowledge about the key policy paradigms. As we have seen, these policy paradigms are sometimes provid-ing very different answers to the same questions. However, it is important to realise that many of these policy approaches have been developed to address the issues of the twentieth century. The world has changed and it is not clear to what extent the old policy paradigms will be able to respond to the challenges of the twenty-first century. However, what is clear is that the world urgently needs policy frameworks that would help to create more balanced, equitable, just and sustainable development for the future. This will not happen overnight and it will not be an easy process. But it is important to realise that it can only happen if everybody contributes to the process. Indeed, we all share a responsibility for the future shape of the economy and society.

And whatever we do, our actions are likely to have implications for thousands of people around the world. As noted numerous times throughout this book, globalisation means increased interconnectedness of human activities – everything we do has an impact on someone else and somewhere else. Globalisation itself, Joseph Stiglitz writes, 'is neither good nor bad' (Stiglitz, 2002, p.20). Importantly, globalisation 'has the *power* to do enormous good' (ibid.; original emphasis). However, the way things are now, there is a growing sense that 'something has gone horribly wrong' (ibid., p.4). According to Stiglitz, it is becoming clear that globali-sation, 'has not succeeded in reducing poverty, neither has it succeeded in ensuring stability' (ibid., p.6). These words of Joe Stiglitz have gained even more currency since the most recent global economic crisis struck. Dealing with the 'Great Recession' (Stiglitz, 2010) is one of the main tasks (see also Box 8.1). In addition to this, it is becoming clear that economic globalisation also poses a global environmental threat. Therefore, it could be argued that economic instability, social and spatial inequality and the threat to the environment are becoming major global (interrelated) issues that need to be tackled in the twenty-first century.

Dicken (2007, p.549) argues that there are three broad possibilities to make the world a better place: to *reform* the present system; to *replace* the present system; or to *diversify* the present system. However, whichever path is chosen, among the big questions that we need to think carefully about are:

- How do we make sure that the global economy will grow in a more stable way?
- How do we make sure that the fruits of this growth will be shared more equitably?
- How do we make sure that the growth of the global economy will not harm the environment and threaten the ecosystem of the entire planet?

In other words, we need to think about the ways in which we can combine economic, social and environmental sustainability. In all three areas, economic geography has a role to play. Indeed, solutions will have to be found at various spatial scales, ranging from the global to the local, and embracing various dimensions from the economic to the social, cultural, political and environmental. Indeed, as Pike et al. (2006, p.256) have argued, progressive models of development are potentially holistic and recognise 'the relations between economic, social, ecological, political and cultural change'. Topics that need to be covered are as diverse as the governance of global finance; international trade relations and ethical trading; investment-related rules; social corporate responsibility; labour standards; re-invigoration of democratic control and participation at various scales; environmental protection; gender issues; cultural identity; intellectual property, and so on. We need a massive debate in all corners of society and all corners of the world about our joint future. I believe that economic geographers have a role to play in such a debate. What is needed, however, is to go beyond the 'new economic geography' to build a conceptual framework that would better reflect economic geographies of the finance-led capitalism in the 'Great Recession' era. In particular, the role of finance, financial capital and the process of financialisation in the (re)production of social and spatial inequalities and economic instability requires urgent attention. In other words, a 'newer' economic geography is needed now.

CONCLUSION

Sometimes the world is described as a 'global village'. However, to paraphrase Lee and Smith (2004) the reality of this 'village' is that of growing fragmentation into sharply divided peoples and places with very unequal life chances. Inequalities that exist at various spatial levels represent a major policy challenge for the twenty-first century. Given that the role of scholarship is not only to understand but also 'to identify and to create a better world' (ibid., p.11), this chapter was designed to open a debate about the policy options for overcoming inequality and uneven development in the globalising world. The chapter provided basic insights into key policy paradigms (neo-liberalism, Keynesianism, socialism, the so-called 'Third Way' and alternative economic approaches), each representing rather different views on the issue of inequality and how the issue should be tackled. Equally, these approaches have different views on the solution to the crisis that recently shook the global economy. However, the world urgently needs to devise new policy frameworks that would contribute to a more balanced, equitable, just and sustainable development for the future. Economic geographers can and should be part of the process via the 'newer' economic geography.

FURTHER READING

Davies, H. (2010) *The Financial Crisis: Who is to Blame?* (Cambridge: Polity Press).

Ellwood, W. (2001) *The No-nonsense Guide to Globalization*. (London: Verso).

Foster, J.B. and F. Magdoff (2009) *The Great Financial Crisis: Causes and Consequences*. (New York: Monthly Review Press).

French, S. and A. Leyshon (2010) '"These F@#king Guys": The Terrible Waste of a Good Crisis', *Environment and Planning A* 42(11), pp.2549–9.

Gamble, A. (2009) *The Spectre at the Feast: Capitalist Crisis and the Politics of Recession.* (Basingstoke and New York: Palgrave Macmillan).

Gibson-Graham, J.K. (2006) *A Post-Capitalist Politics*. (Minneapolis, MN: Minnesota University Press).

Harvey, D. (2005) *A Brief History of Neoliberalism*. (Oxford: Oxford University Press).

Harvey, D. (2010) *The Enigma of Capital and the Crises of Capitalism*. (London: Profile Books).

Krugman, P. (2008) *The Return of Depression Economics and the Crisis of 2008*. (London: Penguin).

Langley, P. (2008) *The Everyday Life of Global Finance: Saving and Borrowing in Anglo-America.* (Oxford and New York: Oxford University Press).

Lee, R. and D.M. Smith (eds) (2004) *Geographies and Moralities: International Perspectives on Development, Justice and Place.* (Oxford: Blackwell).

Lee, R., G. Clark, J. Pollard and A. Leyshon (2009) 'The Remit of Financial Geography – Before and After the Crisis', *Journal of Economic Geography* 9(5), 723–47.

Schwartz, H.M. (2009) *Subprime Nation: American Power, Global Capital, and the Housing Bubble.* (Ithaca and London: Cornell University Press).

Smith, A. and A. Swain (2010) 'The Global Economic Crisis, Eastern Europe, and the Former Soviet Union: Models of Development and the Contradictions of Internationalization', *Eurasian Geography and Economics* 51(1), 1–34.

Stiglitz, J. (2002) *Globalization and its Discontents.* (London: Penguin).

Stiglitz, J. (2007) *Making Globalization Work.* (London: Penguin).

Stiglitz, J. (2010) *Freefall: Free Markets and the Sinking of the Global Economy* (updated edition). (London: Penguin).

Turner, G. (2008) *The Credit Crunch: Housing Bubbles, Globalisation and the Worldwide Economic Crisis.* (London: Pluto Press).

Williams, R. and L. Elliot (eds) (2010) *Crisis and Recovery: Ethics, Economics and Justice.* (Basingstoke: Palgrave Macmillan).

Wolf, M. (2010) *Fixing Global Finance: How to Curb Financial Crises in the 21st Century* (expanded and updated edition). (New Haven and London: Yale University Press).

USEFUL WEBSITES*

http://hdr.undp.org/en/ – website of United Nations Human Development Reports.

http://www.brettonwoodsproject.org/ – website of Bretton Woods Project – critical voices on the World Bank and the IMF.

http://www.ilo.org/global/lang--en/index.htm – website of the International Labour Organization (ILO).

http://www.imf.org/ – website of the International Monetary Fund (IMF).

http://www.undp.org/ – website of the United Nations Development Programme (UNDP).

http://www.worldbank.org/ – website of the World Bank.

http://www.wto.org/index.htm – website of the World Trade Organization (WTO).

http://www.youtube.com/watch?v=hpAMbpQ8J7g – 'First as Tragedy, Then as Farce', an extract from a lecture by a philosopher Slavoj Zizek on ethics in the new cultural capitalism and global inequalities, using coffee as an example (available on YouTube; produced by RSA Animate).

http://www.youtube.com/watch?v=qOP2V_np2c0 – animated lecture of David Harvey on 'Crises of Capitalism' explaining the causes of the global financial crisis from a Marxist perspective (available on YouTube; produced by RSA Animate).

* All accessed 7 March 2011.

Bibliography

Amin, A. (ed.) (1994) *Post-Fordism: A Reader*. (Oxford: Blackwell).

Amin, A. (1999) 'An Institutionalist Perspective on Regional Economic Development', *International Journal of Urban and Regional Research* 23(2), pp.365–78.

Amin, A. and N. Thrift (1992) 'Neo-Marshallian Nodes in Global Networks', *International Journal of Urban and Regional Research* 16(4), pp.571–87.

Amin, A. and N. Thrift (1994) 'Living in the Global', in A. Amin and N. Thrift (eds) *Globalization, Institutions and Regional Development in Europe* (first edition). (Oxford: Oxford University Press), pp.1–22.

Amin, A. and N. Thrift (1995a) 'Institutional Issues for the European Regions: From Markets and Plans to Socioeconomics and Powers of Association', *Economy and Society* 24(1), pp.41–66.

Amin, A. and N. Thrift (1995b) *Globalization, Institutions and Regional Development in European* (new edition). (Oxford: OUP).

Amin, A. and N. Thrift (1999) 'Institutional Issues for the European Regions: From Markets and Plans to Socioeconomics and Powers of Association', in T.J. Barnes and M.S. Gertler (eds) *The New Industrial Geography*. (London and New York: Routledge).

Archibugi, D., J. Howells and J. Michie (eds) (1999) *Innovation Policy in a Global Economy*. (Cambridge: Cambridge University Press).

Asheim, B. (1996) 'Industrial Districts as "Learning Regions": a Condition for Prosperity', *European Planning Studies* 4(4), pp.379–400.

Aydalot, P. and D. Keeble (eds) (1988) *High Technology Industry and Innovative Environments: The European Experience*. (London: Routledge).

Bannock, G., R.E. Baxter and E. Davis (eds) (1998) *The Penguin Dictionary of Economics* (sixth edition). (London and New York: Penguin).

Beaverstock, J.V., R.G. Smith and P.J. Taylor (2000) 'World City Network: A New Metageography?', *Annals of the Association of American Geographers* 90(1), pp.123–34.

Black, J. (ed.) (2002) 'Economy', in *A Dictionary of Economics. (Oxford Reference Online)*. (Oxford: Oxford University Press). Available at: www.oxfordreference.com/views/ENTRY.html?subview=Main&entry=t19.e 944 (subscriber login required); accessed 1 March 2011.

Boekema, F., K. Morgan, S. Bakkers and R. Rutten (eds) (2000) *Knowledge, Innovation and Economic Growth: The Theory and Practice of Learning Regions*. (Cheltenham, UK and Northampton, MA, USA: Edward Elgar).

Braczyk, H.J., P. Cooke and M. Heidenreich (eds) (1998) *Regional Innovation Systems: The Role of Governances in a Globalized World*. (London: UCL Press).

Bradshaw, M. and A. Stenning (eds) (2004) *East Central Europe and the Former Soviet Union: The Post-Socialist States* (London: Prentice Hall).

Bryson, J.R., P.W. Daniels, N. Henry and J. Pollard (eds) (2000) *Knowledge, Space, Economy*. (London and New York: Routledge).

Burton-Jones, A. (1999) *Knowledge Capitalism: Business, Work, and Learning in the New Economy*. (Oxford: Oxford University Press).

Cairncross, F. (1997) *The Death of Distance: How the Communications Revolution Will Change Our Lives*. (London: Orion Business Books).

Camagni, R. (ed.) (1991) *Innovation Networks: Spatial Perspectives*. (London and New York: Belhaven Press).

Castells, M. (1989) *The Informational City: Information Technology, Economic Restructuring and the Urban-regional Process*. (Oxford: Blackwell).

Castells, M. (2000) *The Information Age: Economy, Society and Culture, Vol. I: The Rise of the Network Society* (second edition). (Oxford: Blackwell).

Castells, M. and P. Hall (1994) *Technopoles of the World: The Making of 21st Century Industrial Complexes*. (London: Routledge).

Chant, S. and C. McIlwaine (2009) *Geographies of Development in the 21st Century: An Introduction to the Global South*. (Cheltenham, UK and Northampton, MA, USA: Edward Elgar).

Christaller, W. [1933] (1966) *Central Places in Southern Germany*. (New Jersey: Prentice-Hall).

Clark, G. (2005) 'Money Flows Like Mercury: The Geography of Global Finance', *Geografiska Annaler* 87B(2), pp.99–112.

Clark, G.L., M.P. Feldman and M.S. Gertler (eds) (2003) *The Oxford Handbook of Economic Geography*. (Oxford and New York: Oxford University Press).

Clifford, J.N., S.L. Holloway, S.P. Rice and G. Valentine (eds) (2009) *Key Concepts in Geography* (second edition). (London: Sage).

Clinch, J.P., F.J. Convery and B.M. Walsh (2002) *After the Celtic Tiger: Challenges Ahead*. (Dublin: O'Brien Press).

Coe, N.M., P.F. Kelly and H.W.C. Yeung (2007) *Economic Geography: A Contemporary Introduction*. (Oxford: Blackwell).

Coe, N.M., M. Hess, H.W.C. Yeung, P. Dicken and J. Henderson (2004)

'"Globalizing" Regional Development: A Global Production Networks Perspective', *Transactions of the Institute of British Geographers* 29(4), pp.468–84.

Coffey, W. (1996) 'The "Newer" International Division of Labour', in P.W. Daniels and W.F. Lever (eds) *The Global Economy in Transition*. (Harlow: Longman).

Cohen, R.B, N. Felton, M. Nkosi and J. van Liere (eds) (1979) *The Multinational Corporation: A Radical Approach (Papers by Stephen Herbert Hymer)*. (Cambridge: Cambridge University Press).

Cooke, P. (2002) *Knowledge Economies: Clusters, Learning and Cooperative Advantage*. (London and New York: Routledge).

Cooke, P. and K. Morgan (1994) 'Growth Regions Under Duress: Renewal Strategies in Baden Wurttemberg and Emilia-Romagna', in A. Amin and N. Thrift (eds) *Globalization, Institutions and Regional Development in Europe* (first edition). (Oxford: Oxford University Press), pp.91–117.

Cooke, P. and K. Morgan (1998) *The Associational Economy: Firms, Regions, and Innovation*. (Oxford: Oxford University Press).

Corbridge, S., N.J. Thrift and R. Martin (1994) *Money, Power and Space*. (Oxford: Blackwell).

Craib, I. (1997) *Classical Social Theory: An Introduction to the Thought of Marx, Weber, Durkheim and Simmel*. (Oxford and New York: Oxford University Press).

Davies, H. (2010) *The Financial Crisis: Who is to Blame?* (Cambridge: Polity Press).

Dicken, P. (2003) *Global Shift: Reshaping the Global Economic Map in the 21st Century* (fourth edition). (London: Sage).

Dicken, P. (2007) *Global Shift: Mapping the Changing Contours of the World Economy* (fifth edition). (London: Sage).

Dicken, P. (2011) *Global Shift: Mapping the Changing Contours of the World Economy* (sixth edition). (London: Sage).

Dicken, P. and P. Lloyd (1990) *Location in Space: Theoretical Perspectives in Economic Geography* (third edition). (New York: Harper Collins Publishers).

Dicken, P., J. Peck and A. Tickell (1997) 'Unpacking the Global', in R. Lee and J. Wills (eds) *Geographies of Economies*. (London: Arnold), pp.158–66.

Dunford, M. and A. Smith (2000) 'Catching Up or Falling Behind? Economic Performance and Regional Trajectories in the New Europe', *Economic Geography* 76(2), pp.169–95.

Ellwood, W. (2001) *The No-nonsense Guide to Globalization*. (London: Verso).

Erturk, I., J. Froud, S. Johal, A. Leaver and K. Williams (2008) *Financialization at Work*. (London: Routledge).

Eurostat (2000) 'Central European Candidate Countries: Per Capita GDP below 75% of EU Average in 48 Regions out of 50: Only Prague and Bratislava Matching EU Average', *News Release No 48/2000*, 18 April (Luxembourg: Eurostat).

Farr, J. (2004) 'Social Capital: A Conceptual History', *Political Theory* 32(1), pp.6–33.

Florida, R. (1995) 'Toward the Learning Region', *Futures* 27(5), pp.527–36.

Foster, J.B. and F. Magdoff (2009) *The Great Financial Crisis: Causes and Consequences*. (New York: Monthly Review Press).

French, S. and A. Leyshon (2010) '"These F@#king Guys": The Terrible Waste of a Good Crisis', *Environment and Planning A* 42(11), pp.2549–59.

Fröbel, F., J. Heinrichs and O. Kreye (1980) *The New International Division of Labour*. (Cambridge: Cambridge University Press).

Gamble, A. (2009) *The Spectre at the Feast: Capitalist Crisis and the Politics of Recession*. (Basingstoke and New York: Palgrave Macmillan).

Gereffi, G. (1999) 'International Trade and Industrial Upgrading in the Apparel Commodity Chain', *Journal of International Economics* 48(1), pp.37–70.

Gibson-Graham, J.K. (1996) *The End of Capitalism (As We Knew It): A Feminist Critique of Political Economy*. (Malden, MA: Blackwell).

Gibson-Graham, J.K. (2005) 'Economy', in T. Bennett, L. Grossberg and M. Morris (eds) *New Keywords: A Revised Vocabulary of Culture and Society*. (Malden, MA: Blackwell), pp.95–7.

Gibson-Graham, J.K. (2006) *A Postcapitalist Politics*. (Minneapolis, MN: Minnesota University Press).

Giddens, A. (2000) *The Third Way and its Critics*. (Cambridge: Polity Press).

Gill, I. and B. Quillin (2010) 'Economic Update: The Crisis Hits Home in Emerging Europe', in G. Gorzelak and C.-C. Goh (eds) *Financial Crisis in Central and Eastern Europe: From Similarity to Diversity*. (Warsaw: Wydawnictwo Naukowe Scholar), pp.27–34.

Gill, S. and D. Law (1988) *The Global Political Economy: Perspectives, Problems, and Policies*. (Baltimore: The Johns Hopkins University Press).

Gillespie, A., R. Richardson and J. Cornford (2001) 'Regional Development and the New Economy', *European Investment Bank Papers* 6(1), pp.109–32.

Gorzelak, G. and C.-C. Goh (eds) (2010) *Financial Crisis in Central and*

Eastern Europe: From Similarity to Diversity. (Warsaw: Wydawnictwo Naukowe Scholar).

Graham, S. (1999) 'Global Grids of Glass: On Global Cities, Telecommunications and Planetary Urban Networks', *Urban Studies* 36(5/6), pp.929–49.

Graham, S. and S. Marvin (1996) *Telecommunications and the City: Electronic Spaces, Urban Places*. (London: Routledge).

Grimes, S. (2003) 'Ireland's Emerging Information Economy: Recent Trends and Future Prospects', *Regional Studies* 37(1), pp.3–14.

Grimes, S. and M. White (2005) 'The Transition to Internationally Traded Services and Ireland's Emergence as a "Successful" European Region', *Environment and Planning A* 37(12), pp.2169–88.

Hall, P. and A. Markusen (eds) (1985) *Silicon Landscapes*. (Boston: Allen & Unwin).

Hall, P. and K. Pain (eds) (2006) *The Polycentric Metropolis: Learning From Mega-city Regions in Europe*. (London: Earthscan).

Hamnett, C. (2003) *Unequal City: London in the Global Arena*. (Abingdon: Routledge).

Harper, D. (2001) *Online Etymology Dictionary*. Available at: www.ety monline.com/index.php; accessed 1 March 2011.

Harvey, D. (1978) 'The Urban Process Under Capitalism', *International Journal of Urban and Regional Research* 2(1), pp.101–31.

Harvey, D. (1982) *The Limits to Capital*. (Oxford: Blackwell).

Harvey, D. (1989) *The Condition of Postmodernity: An Enquiry into the Origins of Cultural Change*. (Oxford: Basil Blackwell).

Harvey, D. (2003) *The New Imperialism*. (Oxford: OUP).

Harvey, D. (2005) *A Brief History of Neoliberalism*. (Oxford: Oxford University Press).

Harvey, D. (2006) *The Limits to Capital* (new and fully updated edition). (London and New York: Verso).

Harvey, D. (2010) *The Enigma of Capital and the Crises of Capitalism*. (London: Profile Books).

Held, D. and A. McGrew (eds) (2003a) *The Global Transformations Reader: An Introduction to the Globalization Debate* (second edition). (Cambridge: Polity Press).

Held, D. and A. McGrew (2003b) 'The Great Globalization Debate: An Introduction', in D. Held and A. McGrew (eds) *The Global Transformations Reader: An Introduction to the Globalization Debate* (second edition). (Cambridge: Polity Press), pp.1–50.

Held, D., A. McGrew, D. Goldblatt and J. Perraton (1999) *Global Transformations: Politics, Economics and Culture*. (Cambridge: Polity Press).

Henderson, J., P. Dicken, M. Hess, N. Coe and H.W.C. Yeung (2002) 'Global Production Networks and the Analysis of Economic Development', *Review of International Political Economy* 9(3), pp.436–64.

Hodder, B.W. and R. Lee (1974) *Economic Geography*. (London: Methuen & Co. Ltd).

Hodgson, G.M. (1988) *Economics and Institutions: A Manifesto for a Modern Institutional Economics*. (Cambridge: Polity Press).

Hodgson, G.M. (1993) *Economics and Evolution: Bringing Life Back into Economics*. (Cambridge: Polity Press).

Hodgson, G.M. (1998) 'The Approach of Institutionalist Economics', *Journal of Economic Literature* 36(1), pp.162–92.

Hodgson, G.M. (1999) *Economics and Utopia: Why the Learning Economy is Not the End of History*. (London: Routledge).

Hudson, R. (1999) 'The Learning Economy, the Learning Firm and the Learning Region: a Sympathetic Critique of the Limits to Learning', *European Urban and Regional Studies* 6(1), pp.59–72.

Hudson, R. (2005) *Economic Geographies: Circuits, Flows and Spaces*. (London: Sage).

Hymer, S. (1972) 'The Multinational Corporation and the Law of Uneven Development', in J.N. Bhagwati (ed.) *Economics and World Order: From the 1970's to the 1990's*. (New York: The Free Press), pp.113–40.

IDA (2003) *Ireland, Knowledge is in Our Nature*. (Dublin: IDA Ireland).

Isard, W. (1956) *Location and Space Economy*. (Cambridge, MA: MIT Press).

Ivanička, K. (1996) *Slovakia: Genius Loci*. (Bratislava: Korene Press).

James, A. (2005) 'Demystifying the Role of Culture in Innovative Regional Economies', *Regional Studies* 39(9), pp.1197–216.

James, A. and B. Vira (2009) '"Unionising" the New Spaces of the New Economy? Alternative Labour Organising in India's IT Enabled Services–Business Process Outsourcing Industry', *Geoforum* 41, pp.364–76.

Jones, A. (2006) *Dictionary of Globalization*. (Cambridge: Polity Press).

Kaldor, N. (1970) 'The Case for Regional Policies', *Scottish Journal of Political Economy* 17(3), pp.337–48.

Kaldor, N. (1989) 'The Role of Increasing Returns, Technical Progress and Cumulative Causation in the Theory of International Trade and Economic Growth', in F. Targetti and A. Thirlwall (eds) *The Essential Kaldor*. (London: Duckworth).

Keeble, D. (1989) 'High-technology Industry and Regional Development in Britain: The Case of the Cambridge Phenomenon', *Environment and Planning C: Government and Policy* 7(2), pp.153–72.

Keeble, D. (1992) 'High Technology Industry and the Restructuring of the UK Space Economy', in R. Martin and P. Townroe (eds) *Regional Development in the 1990s: The British Isles in Transition*. (London: Jessica Kingsley Publishers/RSA), pp.172–82.

Kirby, P. (2002) *The Celtic Tiger in Distress: Growth with Inequality in Ireland*. (Basingstoke and New York: Palgrave).

Knox, P. and J. Agnew (1998) *The Geography of the World Economy: An Introduction to Economic Geography* (third edition). (London: Arnold).

Krugman, P. (1991) *Geography and Trade*. (Leuven: Leuven University Press).

Krugman, P. (2003) 'Where in the World is the "New Economic Geography"?', in G.L. Clark, M.P. Feldman and M.S. Gertler (eds) *The Oxford Handbook of Economic Geography*. (Oxford: Oxford University Press), pp.49–60.

Krugman, P. (2008) *The Return of Depression Economics and the Crisis of 2008*. (London: Penguin).

Lagendijk, A. (2000) 'Learning in Non-core Regions: Towards "Intelligent Clusters": Addressing Business and Regional Needs', in F. Boekema, K. Morgan, S. Bakkers and R. Rutten (eds) *Knowledge, Innovation and Economic Growth: The Theory and Practice of Learning Regions*. (Cheltenham, UK and Northampton, MA, USA: Edward Elgar), pp.165–91.

Langley, P. (2008) *The Everyday Life of Global Finance: Saving and Borrowing in Anglo-America*. (Oxford and New York: Oxford University Press).

Leadbeater, C. (2000) *Living on Thin Air: The New Economy*. (London: Penguin Books).

Lee, R. (1994) 'Economic Geography', in R.J. Johnston, D. Gregory and D.M. Smith (eds) *The Dictionary of Human Geography* (third edition). (Oxford: Blackwell), pp.147–54.

Lee, R. (1996) 'Moral Money? LETS and the Social Construction of Local Economic Geographies in Southeast England', *Environment and Planning A* 28(8), pp.1377–94.

Lee, R. (2002a) 'The Economic Importance of Geography', *Financial Times* [London edition], 30 October, p.20.

Lee, R. (2002b) '"Nice Maps, Shame about the Theory"? Thinking Geographically About the Economic', *Progress in Human Geography* 26(3), pp.333–55.

Lee, R. (2006a) 'The Ordinary Economy: Tangled up in Values and Geography', *Transactions of the Institute of British Geographers (New Series)* 31(4), pp.413–32.

Lee, R. (2006b) 'The Ordinary Economy: Tangled Up in Values and

Geography', manuscript. Submitted to the *Transactions of the Institute of British Geographers.*

Lee, R. and D.M. Smith (eds) (2004) *Geographies and Moralities: International Perspectives on Development, Justice and Place.* (Oxford: Blackwell).

Lee, R. and J. Wills (eds) (1997) *Geographies of Economies.* (London: Arnold).

Lee, R., G. Clark, J. Pollard and A. Leyshon (2009) 'The Remit of Financial Geography – Before and After the Crisis', *Journal of Economic Geography* 9(5), 723–47.

Leyshon, A. and R. Lee (2003) 'Introduction: Alternative Economic Geographies', in A. Leyshon, R. Lee and C.C. Williams (eds) *Alternative Economic Spaces.* (London: Sage), pp.1–26.

Leyshon, A. and N.J. Thrift (1997) *Money/Space: Geographies of Monetary Transformation.* (London: Routledge).

Leyshon, A., R. Lee and C.C. Williams (eds) (2003) *Alternative Economic Spaces.* (London: Sage).

Lösh, A. [1935] (1954) *The Economics of Location.* (New Haven, CT: Yale University Press).

Lovering, J. (1999) 'Theory Led by Policy? The Inadequacies of the "New Regionalism" (Illustrated From the Case of Wales)', *International Journal of Urban and Regional Research* 23(2), pp.379–96.

Lundvall, B.A. (1992) *National Innovation Systems: Towards a Theory of Innovation and Interactive Learning.* (London: Pinter).

Lundvall, B.A. and B. Johnson (1994) 'The Learning Economy', *Journal of Industrial Studies* 1(2), pp.23–42.

Lundvall, B.A. and P. Maskell (2003) 'Nation States and Economic Development: From National Systems of Production to National Systems of Knowledge Creation and Learning', in G.L. Clark, M.P. Feldman and M.S. Gertler (eds) *The Oxford Handbook of Economic Geography.* (Oxford: Oxford University Press), pp.353–72.

MacKinnon, D. and A. Cumbers (2007) *An Introduction to Economic Geography: Globalization, Uneven Development and Place.* (Harlow: Pearson/Prentice Hall).

MacKinnon, D., A. Cumbers and K. Chapman (2002) 'Learning, Innovation and Regional Development: A Critical Appraisal of Recent Debates', *Progress in Human Geography* 26(3), pp.293–311.

Malecki, E.J. (2000) 'Creating and Sustaining Competitiveness: Local Knowledge and Economic Geography', in J.R. Bryson, P.W. Daniels, N. Henry and J. Pollard (eds) *Knowledge, Space, Economy.* (London and New York: Routledge), pp.103–19.

Markusen, A., P. Hall, S. Campbell and S. Deitrick (1991) *The Rise of the*

Gunbelt: The Military Remapping of Industrial America. (New York: Oxford University Press).

Marshall, A. [1890] (2009) *Principles of Economics* (unabridged eighth edition). (New York: Cosimo).

Martin, R. (1988) 'The Political Economy of Britain's North–South Divide', *Transactions of the Institute of British Geographers (New Series)* 13(4), pp.389–418.

Martin, R. (1999a) 'The New Economic Geography of Money', in R. Martin (ed.) *Money and the Space Economy.* (Chichester: John Wiley & Sons), pp.3–27.

Martin, R. (ed.) (1999b) *Money and the Space Economy.* (Chichester: John Wiley).

Martin, R. (2002) 'Institutional Approaches in Economic Geography', in E. Sheppard and T.J. Barnes (eds) *A Companion to Economic Geography.* (Malden, MA: Blackwell), pp.77–94.

Martin, R. and P. Sunley (1998) 'Slow Convergence? Post Neo-classical Endogenous Growth Theory and Regional Development', *Economic Geography* 74(3), pp.201–27.

Martin, R. and P. Sunley (2001) 'Rethinking the "Economic" in Economic Geography: Broadening our Vision of Losing our Focus?', *Antipode* 33(2), pp.148–61.

Martin, R. and P. Sunley (2003) 'Deconstructing Clusters: Chaotic Concept or Policy Panacea?', *Journal of Economic Geography* 3(1), pp.5–35.

Maskell, P. and A. Malmberg (1999) 'The Competitiveness of Firms and Regions: "Ubiquitification" and the Importance of Localized Learning', *European Urban and Regional Studies* 6(1), pp.9–25.

Maskell, P., H. Eskelinen, I. Hannibalsson, A. Malmberg and E. Vatne (1998) *Competitiveness, Localised Learning and Regional Development: Specialisation and Prosperity in Small Open Economies.* (London and New York: Routledge).

Massey, D. (1984) *Spatial Divisions of Labour: Social Structures and the Geography of Production.* (London: Macmillan).

Massey, D. (1995) *Spatial Divisions of Labour: Social Structures and the Geography of Production* (second edition). (London: Macmillan).

Massey, D. (2007) *World City.* (Cambridge: Polity).

May, C. (2002) 'Trouble in E-topia: Knowledge as Intellectual Property', *Urban Studies* 39(5–6), pp.1037–49.

May, J., J. Wills, K. Datta, Y. Evans, J. Herbert and C. McIlwaine (2007) 'Keeping London Working: Global Cities, the British State and London's New Migrant Division of Labour', *Transactions of the Institute of British Geographers (New Series)* 32(2), pp.151–67.

Mohan, J. (1999) *A United Kingdom?: Economic, Social and Political Geographies*. (London: Arnold).

Morgan, K. (1997) 'The Learning Region: Institutions, Innovation and Regional Renewal', *Regional Studies* 31(5), pp.491–503.

Morgan, K. (1998) 'Regional Renewal: The Development Agency as Animateur', in H. Halkier, M. Danson and C. Damborg (eds) *Regional Development Agencies in Europe*. (London: Jessica Kingsley Publishers/ RSA), pp.229–52.

Myrdal, G. (1957) *Economic Theory and Underdeveloped Regions*. (London: Harper & Row).

Nelson, R. and S. Winter (1982) *An Evolutionary Theory of Economic Change*. (Cambridge, MA: Harvard University Press).

O'Brien, R. (1992) *Global Financial Integration: The End of Geography*. (London: Royal Institute of International Affairs).

OECD (1996) *Regional Problems and Policies in the Czech Republic and the Slovak Republic*. (Paris: OECD).

O'Gorman, C. and M. Kautonen (2004) 'Policies to Promote New Knowledge-intensive Industrial Agglomerations', *Entrepreneurship and Regional Development* 16(6), pp.459–79.

Ó Gráda, C. (1997) *A Rocky Road: The Irish Economy Since the 1920s*. (Manchester and New York: Manchester University Press).

O'Hogan, J.W. (ed.) (2000) *The Economy of Ireland: Policy and Performance of a European Region.* (Dublin: Gill & Macmillan Ltd.).

Pacione, M. (2005) *Urban Geography: A Global Perspective* (second edition). (Abingdon: Routledge).

Peck, J. and N. Theodore (2007) 'Variegated Capitalism', *Progress in Human Geography* 31(6), pp.731–72.

Perrons, D. (2004) *Globalization and Social Change: People and Places in a Divided World*. (Abingdon: Routledge).

Pickles, J. and A. Smith, (eds) (1998) *Theorising Transition: The Political Economy of Post-Communist Transformations.* (London: Routledge).

Pike, A., A. Rodriguez-Pose and J. Tomaney (2006) *Local and Regional Development*. (London and New York: Routledge).

Piore, M. and C. Sabel (1984) *The Second Industrial Divide: Possibilities for Prosperity*. (New York: Basic Books).

Porter, M. (2000) 'Locations, Clusters and Company Strategy', in G.L. Clark, M.P. Feldman and M.S. Gertler (eds) *The Oxford Handbook of Economic Geography*. (Oxford: Oxford University Press), pp.253–74.

Potter, R.B., T. Binns, J.A. Elliot and D. Smith (2004) *Geographies of Development*. (Harlow: Pearson/Prentice Hall).

Regan, C. (ed.) (2002) *80:20 Development in an Unequal World*. (Wicklow: 80:20 Educating and Acting for a Better World).

Reinhart, C.M. and K.S. Rogoff, (2009) *This Time is Different: Eight Centuries of Financial Folly*. (Princeton and Oxford: Princeton University Press).

Sassen, S. (2001) *The Global City: New York, London, Tokyo* (second edition). (Princeton and Oxford: Princeton University Press).

Saxenian, A. (1996) *Regional Advantage: Culture and Competition in Silicon Valley and Route 128* (new edition). (Cambridge and London: Harvard University Press).

Schwartz, H.M. (2009) *Subprime Nation: American Power, Global Capital, and the Housing Bubble*. (Ithaca and London: Cornell University Press).

Scott, A.J. (1988) *New Industrial Spaces: Flexible Production Organisation and Regional Development in North America and Western Europe*. (London: Pion).

Shaik, A. (1991) 'Economic Crisis', in T. Bottomore (ed.) *A Dictionary of Marxist Thought* (second edition). (Oxford: Blackwell), pp.160–65.

Smith, A. (1776) *An Inquiry into the Nature and Causes of the Wealth of Nations*. Read the work of Adam Smith online via The Library of Economics and Liberty. Available at: www.econlib.org/library/Smith/smWN.html; accessed 1 March 2011.

Smith, A. (1998) *Reconstructing the Regional Economy: Industrial Transformation and Regional Development in Slovakia*. (Cheltenham, UK and Lyme, NH, USA: Edward Elgar).

Smith, A. (2002) 'Imagining Geographies of the "New Europe": Geo-economic Power and the New European Architecture of Integration', *Political Geography* 21(5), pp.647–70.

Smith, A. and A. Rochovská (2006) 'Neo-liberalism and "Post-socialist" Urban Transformations: Poverty, Inequality and the City', *Acta Geographica* 48, pp.43–54.

Smith, A. and A. Rochovská (2007) 'Domesticating Neo-liberalism: Everyday Lives and the Geographies of Post-socialist Transformations', *Geoforum* 38(6), pp.1163–78.

Smith, A. and A. Swain (2010) 'The Global Economic Crisis, Eastern Europe, and the Former Soviet Union: Models of Development and the Contradictions of Internationalization', *Eurasian Geography and Economics* 51(1), 1–34.

Smith, A., A. Stenning, A. Rochovská and D. Swiatek (2008) 'The Emergence of a Working Poor: Labour Markets, Neoliberalisation and Diverse Economies in Post-socialist Cities', *Antipode* 40(2), pp.283–311.

Smith, A., A. Rainnie, M. Dunford, J. Hardy, R. Hudson and D. Sadler (2002) 'Networks of Value, Commodities and Regions: Reworking

Divisions of Labour in Macro-regional Economies', *Progress in Human Geography* 26(1), pp.41–63.

Smith, D.M. (1994a) 'Agglomeration', in R.J. Johnston, D. Gregory and D.M. Smith (eds) *The Dictionary of Human Geography* (third edition). (Oxford: Blackwell), p.4.

Smith, D.M. (1994b) 'External Economies', in R.J. Johnston, D. Gregory and D.M. Smith (eds) *The Dictionary of Human Geography* (third edition). (Oxford: Blackwell), pp.184–5.

Smith, N. (1984) *Uneven Development: Nature, Capital and the Production of Space*. (Oxford: Basil Blackwell).

Soanes, C. and A. Stevenson (eds) (2006) 'Economy', in *The Concise Oxford English Dictionary* (revised eleventh edition). (Oxford: Oxford University Press/Oxford Reference Online). Available at: www.oxfordreference.com/views/ENTRY.html?subview=Main&entry=t23.
e17581 (subscriber login required); accessed 1 March 2011.

Sokol, M. (2001) 'Central and Eastern Europe a Decade after the Fall of State-Socialism: Regional Dimensions of Transition Processes', *Regional Studies* 35(7), pp.645–55.

Sokol, M. (2003) 'Regional Dimensions of the Knowledge Economy: Implications for the "New Europe"' (University of Newcastle upon Tyne: Unpublished PhD Thesis).

Sokol, M. (2004) 'The "Knowledge Economy": a Critical View', in P. Cooke and A. Piccaluga (eds) (2004) *Regional Economies as Knowledge Laboratories*. (Cheltenham, UK and Northampton, MA, USA: Edward Elgar), pp.216–31.

Sokol, M. (2007) 'Space of Flows, Uneven Regional Development and the Geography of Financial Services in Ireland', *Growth and Change* 38(2), pp.224–59.

Sokol, M. (2009), 'Regional Connectivity', in R. Kitchin and N. Thrift (eds) *International Encyclopedia of Human Geography*, Volume 9. (Oxford: Elsevier), pp.165–80.

Stiglitz, J. (2002) *Globalization and its Discontents*. (London: Penguin).

Stiglitz, J. (2007) *Making Globalization Work*. (London: Penguin).

Stiglitz, J. (2010) *Freefall: Free Markets and the Sinking of the Global Economy* (updated edition). (London: Penguin).

Storper, M. (1995) 'The Resurgence of Regional Economies, Ten Years Later: the Region as a Nexus of Untraded Interdependencies', *European Urban and Regional Studies* 2(3), pp.191–221.

Storper, M. (1997) *The Regional World: Territorial Development in a Global Economy*. (New York and London: Guilford Press).

Storper, M. (1999) 'The Resurgence of Regional Economies: Ten Years Later', in J. Barnes and M. Gertler (eds) *The New Industrial*

Geography: Regions, Regulation and Institutions. (London and New York: Routledge), pp.23–53.

Storper, M. and A.J. Scott (1995) 'The Wealth of Regions', *Futures* 27(5), pp.505–26.

Taylor, P. (2004) *World City Network: A Global Urban Analysis*. (London and New York: Routledge).

Thornhill, J. (2009) 'Agitation as Middle-class Europe Struggles to Cope', *Financial Times*, 12 March, p. 17.

Tickell, A. (2005) 'Money and Finance', in P. Cloke, P. Crang and M. Goodwin (eds) *Introducing Human Geographies* (second edition). (Abingdon: Hodder Arnold), pp.244–52.

Trend (1993) 'Kde sa v Europe oplati investovat', *Trend-Fakt*, 22 September, pp.1–3.

Turner, G. (2008) *The Credit Crunch: Housing Bubbles, Globalisation and the Worldwide Economic Crisis*. (London: Pluto Press).

UNDP (2001) *Human Development Report 2001 (Making New Technologies Work for Human Development)*. United Nations Development Programme (UNDP). (New York: Oxford University Press).

UNDP (2007) *Human Development Report 2007/2008 (Fighting Climate Change: Human Solidarity in a Divided World)*. United Nations Development Programme (UNDP). (Basingstoke and New York: Palgrave Macmillan).

von Thünen, J.H. [1826] (1966) *Der Isolierte Staat* (volumes I, II, III originally published in 1826, 1850, 1867) in P. Hall (ed.) *Von Thunen's Isolated State*. (Oxford: Pergamon).

Weber, A. (1929) *Theory of the Location of Industries*. (Chicago: University of Chicago Press).

White, M. and S. Grimes (2004) 'Placing Ireland's Transition to a Knowledge Economy within a Global Context', in P. Cooke and A. Piccaluga (eds) *Regional Economies as Knowledge Laboratories*. (Cheltenham, UK and Northampton, MA, USA: Edward Elgar), pp.161–80.

Williams, R. (1976) *Keywords: A Vocabulary of Culture and Society*. (London: Fontana/Croom Helm).

Williams, R. and L. Elliot (eds) (2010) *Crisis and Recovery: Ethics, Economics and Justice*. (Basingstoke: Palgrave Macmillan).

Williamson, O.E. (1975) *Markets and Hierarchies: Analysis and Anti-trust Implications: A Study in the Economics of Internal Organization*. (New York: Free Press).

Wills, J. (2001) *Mapping Low Pay in East London*. Queen Mary, University of London. Available at: http://www.york.ac.uk/res/fbu/documents/mlpinel_sep2001.pdf; accessed 7 March 2011.

Wills, J., K. Datta, Y. Evans, J. Herbert, J. May and C. McIlwaine (2009) *Global Cities at Work: New Migrant Divisions of Labour*. (London and New York: Pluto Press).

Wilson, M.I. and K.E. Corey (eds) (2000) *Information Tectonics: Space, Place and Technology in an Electronic Age*. (New York: John Wiley & Sons).

Wolf, M. (2004) *Why Globalization Works*. (London; New Haven: Yale University Press).

Wolf, M. (2010) *Fixing Global Finance: How to Curb Financial Crises in the 21st Century* (expanded and updated edition). (New Haven and London: Yale University Press).

Wolff, R.D. and S.A. Resnick (1987) *Economics: Marxian Versus Neoclassical*. (Baltimore and London: The Johns Hopkins University Press).

World Bank (2010) *The Crisis Hits Home: Stress-testing Households in Europe and Central Asia*. (Washington: IBRD/The World Bank). Available at: www.worldbank.org; accessed 7 March 2011.

Index